THE STORY OF
TAIZÉ

J. L. Gonzalez Balado

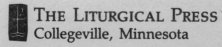

THE LITURGICAL PRESS
Collegeville, Minnesota

Published in the United States of America by
The Liturgical Press
Collegeville, Minnesota 56321

First English Language Edition
(revised and updated) published 1980
by Mowbray, Villiers House,
41/47 Strand,
London WC2N 5JE, a Cassell Company

New revised edition: 1981
Second revised edition: 1985
Third revised edition: 1988
Reprinted with revisions: 1990

Typeset by Acorn Bookwork, Salisbury, Wilts
Printed in Great Britain by
Richard Clay Ltd, Bungay, Suffolk

First published in Spanish: *El Desafío de Taizé*, by
Ediçiones Paulinas, Madrid
First edition: May 1976
Second edition: March 1978

Editions in:

French (Seuil, Paris 1976)
Italian (EP, Rome-Turin 1976)
Portuguese (Ediçiones Paulinas, San Paolo 1977)
German (Herder Verlag, Freiburg im Breisgau 1977)

ISBN 0 8146 2017 5

Contents

*'One passes through Taizé as one
passes close to a spring of water.'*

John Paul II

Echoes

IT IS five o'clock on a hot afternoon in August 1987. We are out in the country, on a hillside in eastern France. Several hundred people are gathered in 'Tent A', a large marquee set up in a field between the Church of Reconciliation and the Yellow House. They are listening to a group of young Indians whose words are being translated simultaneously into French, Italian, Spanish, Finnish, Polish and probably other languages as well. It is tea-time during the 'intercontinental meetings' which, throughout this summer, have brought together in this village of Taizé young adults from the world over.

Across the way, in a similar tent, another crowd is listening to some young Africans. Every afternoon at five, people stop for a cup of tea during a busy day of Bible introductions, small-group sharing, prayer and silent reflection, and practical work. This is a time for those who have come from farthest away to share something of their country, their faith, their own hopes and those of their people. They have come from South Africa and Zaire, from Chile and Peru, from Haiti, from the North-West of Thailand. . . .

Here in Tent A, the speakers are from South India. 'Tamilnadu is known for the wealth of its Hindu tradition,' says Mary Agnes. 'Yet it has also been a cradle for the Indian Church, thanks to St Thomas the apostle, who came to preach the Gospel in Tamilnadu. He was martyred on St Thomas Mount, which is our parish.'

'As you know, the first Taizé intercontinental meeting was held in Madras,' continues Sharon. 'Together with the

1

brothers of Taizé, the young people had been preparing the meeting for over a year. The preparation brought together Christians of all denominations – Catholics, Church of South India, Lutherans, Syrian Orthodox, all working together. The meeting was unique because not only Christians took part, but we also had a lot of Hindus and Muslims.

'For us in India, it was a great opportunity to meet young Christians from all over the world. It gave us a world view of the Church. Now we have parts of our families all over the world and that makes it more personal. And there was the presence of the many Asians, from Japan, Korea, Thailand, Cambodia, Malaysia and Australia. Taizé also brought the different Churches of Madras together. For example, in my parish we have the Catholic church and the CSI church side by side. But there had never been any common activities, and so this was something unique for the young people working together for the meeting – the opportunity to build true lasting friendship. We have a long way to travel, for as you know Christians only form two per cent of the population; but now we know we'll travel together.'

When Sharon finishes, John Bosco begins to explain about their parish of Shastrinagar, one of the poorest neighbourhoods in India. The people are Tamils who had been taken to Burma by the British, and were unwanted in Burma after the independence of that country. In 1962 they settled in Madras, receiving permission to build huts next to a big pond collecting waste water from the city. Tensions between Hindus and Christians soon broke out, and the young people wanted to do something about them: 'During the preparation of the Madras meeting we never got any support from our elders, because they thought we would land in trouble with our Hindu brothers. But we continued and said to them, "No, we youngsters will build and develop ourselves and have peace among us in the future." The Madras meeting was fortunately a turning-point for us.

2

We prepared a tent to invite our friends from Europe and other parts. The very moment they were with us, the elders felt something extraordinary was happening and started to support us. That brought unity between the elders and the youngsters which still lasts. . . .'

Six o'clock struck, and tea-time was over. People went off for different meetings and activities. I walked back to El Abiodh, the guest-house, with Sharon, and I asked her how long she had been in Taizé. 'Two months, almost two and a half. First I joined the group discussions, then I went into silence for a while. Since then I have spent time helping out, working with young people from different countries. I especially liked working with the young families with children; it made me homesick for my country, the family atmosphere and all. And then with children you don't need to worry about what language you speak.'

As we walked along the road Sharon told me more about herself. 'I've just finished my university course, in management. So when I go back I will have to choose what I want to do. It's an important time. Many young people in India have a tendency to idolise the West, not to be conscious of the richness of their own country. I didn't realise this before, why we were told so often at college not to imitate the West. I thought it was silly at the time. I guess you have to go away in order to appreciate what you have.'

We sat down in the garden of El Abiodh, where some of the Sisters of St Andrew were sitting on the grass in deep conversation with young women. I asked Sharon how she became involved with Taizé. 'Actually, I met the sisters first; they came over to the retreat centre where I was working and spoke to us. It was the international year of youth, and so I was excited to hear that a huge meeting was going to be held right here in Madras. But at first I didn't understand the meaning of the preparation. I used to get a little impatient sometimes: "When are they going to talk about action? They go on talking about looking for signs of hope!" During the meeting I was very busy. I had to rush to the parish to get things organised there and then go back to Loyola College to welcome the participants. I would leave my house at five-thirty in the morning and get back at eleven at night, but it was enjoyable. It was nice to welcome others to Madras.'

Sharon then spoke of her stay in Europe. 'It was very important for those of us who came from far away to have had the opportunity to visit parishes in Europe. I realised then how truly I am a messenger, an ambassador from one Church to another. Not only do you discover the life of the Church in the parishes you visit, but in a way you are confirmed in your own faith back home by sharing it with others. When people don't understand, you try to explain it and then you understand it yourself more.' She had visited Italy as part of a team of six: two from South America, two from Zambia, and two Indians: 'It was wonderful, a constant comparison of our attitudes, and the life together with the Italians. And then there was a prayer service in Turin with about five hundred young people from different cities. They had taken the pews out, and we had the prayer around the Cross. I was touched to find a little piece of Taizé there. And all the time, I felt supported by the Churches of Madras. I had so many messages saying we were together in prayer. Then I realised who my true friends were.'

Different, yet alike

It was time for the evening meal, and so I said goodbye to Sharon. Her words had brought back to me another conversation held almost fifteen years earlier on that same hillside. Alison was from England; she had just finished her studies in literature and had decided to take a year off, 'in order to go more into things', as she put it. She would spend the time

4

in Taizé helping to welcome people and to lead discussion groups. Later on she went with young people to West Africa, to visit groups and parishes in Kenya, Tanzania and Zambia and to spend two months living in a poor part of Nairobi. She had also told me about her work setting up with others an 'open house' in central Bristol, welcoming those with no place to go, and her involvement in the housing problems there.

I was musing on this similarity between two people so far apart in time and place, and how the unique vocation of this community of brothers here made possible this discovery of a similarity, when I happened to bump into Tim. Tim is an eighteen-year-old American of infectious good humour who had spent the last eighteen months in Taizé to help with the work of welcoming and taking care of the many visitors. Earlier I had asked him about his own journey and the role Taizé played in it, and he let me read an essay he had recently written on that very question:

'In the fall of 1985, I was fairly convinced I was "on my way". But to where? I had survived four years of high school with only minor mishaps and been accepted to a prestigious university. I was possibly on my way to creating a self-image shared by many of today's young people, in America and abroad. The image of the young and successful champion of the status quo, honed for competition; a self-oriented and conscienceless consumer, a "winner", that priceless commodity in a performance society.

'I had come to France, to quote Thomas Merton, for a goal probably not too different from that of "most people" in their search for happiness: "to grab everything and see everything and investigate every experience and then talk about it". Fortunately, several obstacles would appear in my path before I would reach that goal.

'Taizé: when I first climbed the winding footpath that leads to the village, it was December 20th of last year: I had

5

little idea of what to expect, save for some vaguely romantic notion of spending Christmas in a monastery. Only now am I able to verbalize, to communicate what began in those two weeks. They marked the beginning of a spiritual search, a continuing experience of discovery.

'The first thing that impressed me was the life of the brothers themselves – a simple life of prayer, work and communion in the spirit of the great monastic traditions. Far from polemics and referendums, they attempt to be a living sign of reconciliation in the spirit of the Beatitudes: Joy, Simplicity and Mercy.

'Secondly, there was the experience of making contact with the thousands of visitors who come to take part in the meetings, so many of whom have taken the initiative to *do something* for others. Each one has a unique testimony of struggle and faith that opens our perspective to what lies beyond our immediate reality.

'Finally, there is what may be termed the spirit of pilgrimage. Each of us, from a different milieu, with a different perspective, with little in common save for the shared hope in a common destination. It is at that point that each one is called, in the words of Micah, to "seek justice, to love goodness, and to walk humbly with your God".

'During my stay in Taizé, the combination of these three things was able to germinate and take root in my spirit: when I returned in March, the essential re-evaluation of my values and motivations had been done. The living example of those who have chosen simplicity, who have accepted the challenge to live at the service of others, was a greater indictment of my own self-centred life than all the words I have ever heard. I felt the need for a radical departure from the life in which I craved sophistication rather than simplicity and chose competition over reconciliation.

'If someone were to ask me, "What have you found at Taizé?", I would have to call on the eloquence of Gerard

Manley Hopkins: "I have found the dominant of my range and state". I have found the desire to be a presence of simplicity and contemplation in the midst of a hectic world; I have found a sense of purpose and direction.' ✎——

'My trust in the young'

We have just listened to echoes from young people from three continents separated by almost fifteen years, yet beyond the differences of time and place, the accents are the same. A Polish philosopher, struck by this continuity, recently expressed it this way:

'Not too many years ago, were we not witnesses to a wave of protest against an oppressive and soulless world? Groups, communities, movements sprang up everywhere; young people broke with the world and went looking for a different life-style. Some wanted to change the world, others simply wanted to drop out and live in their own way. Their destinies were various. Most of them became weary, discouraged and dispersed; they became conformists again. But on the map of the world, there is one place that began to attract young adults in ever-growing numbers, searching for something different, for another kind of life. It was a community whose members had no grandiose plans of action and who never expected the arrival of so many pilgrims. Who are they? "A group of men who did not choose one another and who want to live out something of the life of the first Christian community." They want to pray and search for God, to be a sign of unity among Christians. More and more people have come to visit them, especially the young. The visitors began to ask questions and to join them in prayer. The brothers tried above all to listen to them, to help them find a way.'

Two visions of Taizé; a community that prays, rooting all its life in contemplation, and a place where the generations

7

meet, where the young are made welcome. Hundreds of thousands of them have come to Taizé in the last twenty-five years, from all the countries of Europe and beyond, and the numbers show no signs of decreasing. How did this come about? To understand something we generally look for comparisons, and Taizé has been compared with all kinds of other places. It is my belief that Taizé, by its history and personality, cannot be compared with anything that exists at present, nor with anything the past has known. As for the future, all you can say is that if one day 'something like Taizé' arises, it will be completely different! Taizé was born and lives in constant movement; it is all the time passing from one provisional form to another, different one. In 1965 the founder of Taizé, Brother Roger, wrote a book called *The Dynamic of the Provisional*, and that attitude has always been crucial for the community. It is also implicit in another of Brother Roger's early works, *Living Today for God*, out of which the BBC was to draw the title for a first-class film on a moment of Taizé's life, 'A Place for Today'.

All the books written by Brother Roger are marked by this concern for 'today'. In recent years, the founder of Taizé has published several volumes of excerpts from his daily journal, together with longer meditations on some particular Gospel theme. In addition, to help the young 'find a way', to accompany many others, young and old, on their life-long pilgrimage, Brother Roger writes an open letter at the end of each year. He begins this task months ahead of time, noting the questions young people ask in the hours he spends listening to them, paying attention to their hopes and their difficulties. Then, in the course of several weeks, he composes a letter which will be made public during a large 'European meeting'. To ensure that the ideas it contains are indeed universal, and to take the harsh realities of the world into account, he often finishes the letter while sharing the living conditions of the poorest of

8

the poor somewhere in the world. The letter is then given the name of the place where it was brought to a conclusion: the *Letter from Haiti*, written in 1983 after a stay in a large shanty-town in Port-au-Prince; the *Letter from the Desert*, written in sub-Saharan Africa in 1984, at a time of drought and famine; the *Letter from Madras*, finished in 1985 during days spent in a poor section of that Indian metropolis.

During the entire year, the new letter is the basis for reflection during all the meetings held in Taizé and elsewhere. It is generally translated into more than twenty languages. Writing a letter each year is a way of responding to the questions asked by each new generation, of attempting to express Gospel truths in the language of today. These past years, many young people have experienced feelings of indifference and discouragement, and so the letters often include a reminder that it is still possible to hope, as in this excerpt from the *Letter from Madras*:

'If you are dismayed by the mistrust that exists between nations and by the wounds left by broken human relationships, will you let your lips and your heart become frozen in an attitude of "What's the use, we can do nothing, let things take their course".

'Are you going to let yourself sink into discouragement like Elijah, a believer of times gone by, who, seeing that he could do nothing more for his people, lay down under a tree to fall asleep and forget?

'Or will you remain awake? you have a long journey ahead of you. Will you take your place among those women, men and children who have decided to act?

'They possess unexpected strengths. By their very simplicity, their lives speak to us. They foster sharing and solidarity, and dispel the paralysis of indifference. They disarm mistrust and hatred. They are bearers of trust and reconciliation.'

'Bearers of trust and reconciliation.' In these words I seem to hear an echo of Brother Roger's own life, and the life of the community he began. If Taizé is a place where countless people, young and old, have discovered afresh these Gospel values, the roots of this are perhaps to be sought in the founder of Taizé's own inner journey. Others have recognised this as well. In 1974, Brother Roger was awarded the prestigious Templeton Prize, given to a person of whatever faith who, in the opinion of the jury, had done most to foster in others a greater 'knowledge and love of God'. Although he gave away the sum of money attached to the prize to young people working for reconciliation, he did go to London to receive the award at the hands of Prince Philip. Speaking at the Guildhall afterwards, he said: 'I would go to the uttermost ends of the earth, to the world's farthest end, to tell over and over again that I trust the new generations, that I trust the young. We who are older must listen, and never condemn. Listen, always listen, to grasp the very best of the creative intuitions alive in the hearts of today's youth. They are going to open up paths . . . and draw the whole People of God in their train.'

That same year, speaking to an assembly in the Pauluskirche in Frankfurt, Germany, after being named 'Man of Peace, 1974', Brother Roger explained more fully the origins of this vocation to trust and listening in his own youth. He made more explicit reference to his past than he usually does. It is only fitting that the last of our echoes should be of this early, decisive moment:

'When I was young, at a time when humanity was being torn apart, I kept on asking myself: why these conflicts, these categorical condemnations of people by one another, even among Christians? And I wondered if in fact a way existed by which one person might understand another completely. And one day (I know its date) in a spot I could describe, with the soft light of evening, the countryside

10

vanishing in the twilight, I made a decision. I said to myself: assume that that way does exist. Now begin with yourself and commit yourself, you at any rate, to understand everything of every other person. On that day I knew for sure that the resolve I had made would be definitive, that it would last until I died. It would involve a constant return, all through my life, to that once-for-all decision. I would try to understand everything, rather than try to make others understand me.'

Beginnings

NOW, WE have to try to begin at the beginning. But where are we going to set a beginning? We have just seen, at the end of the last chapter, a decision which is a real beginning. That resolve 'to understand others rather than try to make others understand me' opens a lifetime of comprehension, of kindness and mercy. Should the beginning be set in 1940, when Roger arrived in Taizé for the first time? Or in 1949, when the first seven brothers bound themselves for a whole lifetime in community? Or at Roger's birth? In one sense, 6 November 1958 is a beginning. Only a few days before, on 28 October, the whole world had been asking the same question: 'But who is he?' A few weeks previously Pius XII had been laid to rest; then, on that Wednesday afternoon, Cardinal Canali had emerged from the conclave to announce 'a great joy: we have a Pope!' Perhaps he too found it odd to have to announce a name that nobody was expecting to hear: a man in his seventy-seventh year, Cardinal Angelo Giuseppe Roncalli, Patriarch of Venice, once nuncio in Paris. Pope John – the twenty-third of that name, and who remembers the other twenty-two? 'A Pope of transition!'

At Rome, one cardinal was particularly anxious to spend a few moments with the new Pope. Cardinal Gerlier of Lyon was old and sensed that he did not have long to live. Two concerns had always been of vital importance for him: Christian unity and social justice. Now, at the end of his life, he wanted to bequeath those concerns to the new Pope. Nobody, he felt, would be better able to help him in this than the founder and prior of Taizé. So at the end of the audience, Cardinal Gerlier asked Pope John to see Brother

Roger. The Pope agreed readily, laying down a condition which shows how new he felt in his task: the issues raised were not to be too difficult for him.

So the morning of 6 November, only two days after the papal coronation, Brother Roger and Brother Max in their white robes approached the door where John XXIII came forward to meet them. We can be sure that it was as warm an encounter as all the audiences with John XXIII seem to have been. It was the beginning of a series of audiences, and of friendship. Two years later, the Pope was to greet the brothers with, 'Ah, Taizé – that little springtime!' The beginning too of other adventures. . . .

Roger Louis Schutz-Marsauche

His mother, Amélie Marsauche, was French, from northern Burgundy. His father, Charles Schutz, was of a family from the Swiss Jura, where he and Amélie settled after their marriage. He was a pastor. The family of Amélie was equally a line of pastors, and their engagement was the result of an agreement between the two families, in the fashion of the time. They had seven daughters and two sons; Roger was their last child. He was born in the little village of Provence, fifteen miles from Neuchâtel, on 12 May 1915; his father was pastor there. He was given a double name but the second part never left the pages of the baptismal register. He was always 'Roger', and it is a name he loves. In one of his books he explains how his seven sisters gathered to choose that name for him.

Of his father Brother Roger has written, 'I admired him for his courage. Like my mother, he demanded authenticity, truthfulness of us in our lives.' Another memory is surely of great significance, in view of what his son was to become. 'I am sure that my father was a mystic at heart. Very early in the morning, he would go to pray alone in church. Once, when I was twelve, I even saw him go into a Catholic church. All the boys in the village were there and saw him go in, pray in silence and have no comment to make about the fact when he came out. That struck me.'

It is clear that already as a child, Roger looked beyond the divisions between 'Catholic' and 'Protestant'. Today he often speaks in this regard of the decisive role played by his maternal grandmother: 'During the Great War, she was a widow living in the North of France. Her three sons were at the front. Although bombs were falling close by, she refused to leave her home. She opened her door to refugees – old people, children, pregnant women, only leaving at the very last minute. My grandmother wanted no one ever again to have to experience what she had gone through. Christians were killing one another in Europe. If only they could be reconciled, perhaps another war could be avoided. Although she was from a family that had been Protestant for generations, in order to achieve a reconciliation within herself, she used to visit a Catholic church. It was as if she had somehow realised that, in the Catholic Church, the Eucharist is a source of unanimity of the faith. The miracle of her life was that in reconciling within herself the faith in which she had been brought up with, the faith of the Catholic Church, she was able to live in such a way that she did not appear to repudiate her own people.'

Through these and other memories scattered throughout his writings, we gain a picture of Roger growing up in the difficult position of 'the pastor's son' in a large family where financial worries played their part, and learning an openness, adaptability and discretion that were later going to come into their own. Charles Schutz was not to see that day. He died suddenly in March 1946, at a moment when he could only ponder the risks his son had taken. 'How are you going to survive materially in the enterprise you have begun? How will you ever manage to earn your living in

14

Taizé?' Such were the questions preoccupying him when he and Roger spoke for the last time. His widow was to live many years longer, dying in December 1973 at the age of ninety-three. For many years she had been living in Taizé. At the end of her life she was heard to say, 'I love life. I'm not afraid to die; I know where I am going; I know in whom I believe.' The day she died she said, 'Let us remain joyful. . . . Life is wonderful.' Several times she repeated, '*Jésus . . . c'est beau!*' Those were her last words; she is buried in the churchyard at Taizé.

Roger the 'agnostic'

When Roger was about thirteen, he had to leave home to attend a secondary school in a town some distance away. 'It meant finding me lodgings in the town, and my parents had the choice of two families, one Protestant and the other Catholic. The latter family was poor, a widow with many children who had lost everything on the death of her husband. My parents felt that the income from my rent for lodging there might be a help, although they had some hesitations, since she was not of their Church. But generosity won the day, so I lived those childhood years in two families, one Protestant, the other Catholic.' For Brother Roger, those two families which were both 'his' explain much about the shape his ecumenical vocation was to take.

During those secondary-school years, Roger experienced a deep crisis of faith. 'For several years I was not a believer. Yet, without having faith myself, I was always full of respect for those who did believe – like the young people I see today.' When Brother Roger now speaks of those years, he tends to see in them a period of 'agnosticism', or of 'not-being-able-to-say-I-believe', rather than of radical disbelief. Lengthy discussions between him and Madame Bioley, his Catholic landlady, always revolved around the question of belief, how it is possible? 'She left an indelible mark on me,' Roger was to recall. 'She was a living expression of the Gospel's sovereign freedom.' Alone, he continued to spend time in church, in silence.

During those years, Roger was to discover a chapter of French religious history which has no parallel in English-speaking Christendom: Pascal and Port-Royal. It would be hard to overestimate the role played in his life by that discovery. The whole family adored reading aloud, and long months were consecrated to the history of Port-Royal by Sainte-Beuve. In addition, Roger could always see on his mother's desk a portrait of Mother Angélique Arnaud, whom his mother referred to as her 'invisible friend'. It was not Jansenism that attracted Roger, but the beauty of an intense community life lived at Port-Royal, and the fact that just a few women, committing themselves to the full, were able to have such an impact on so many others. In the same way, it is not the violently polemical Pascal of certain writings that appealed to him, but the Pascal who knows what it is to doubt, who struggles and opts for the risk of happiness that only God can give. Not proof, but inklings and 'the reasons the heart has which reason cannot know'.

We only realise the full extent of this crisis when we know that at the same moment Roger was struck down with tuberculosis. Consumption was still a dangerous disease; his long convalescence, filled with reading and thinking, brought a gradual return to the surface – to life again, but also to a measure of serenity, of inner peace.

What now?

By the time he was twenty, Roger had his school life and the crisis of adolescence behind him. Now was the moment to decide on the next step. In his father's mind, there was no doubt that he should go on to study theology. Roger, however, seems to have been strongly attracted to more literary studies: 'I dreamed of being a writer and farmer.' During his long months of illness, he had begun to write, and the result was an essay entitled 'Evolution of a Puritan Boyhood'. He decided to offer it for publication in the *Nouvelle Revue Française*, and one day he left for Paris without telling his father the real reason behind his journey. There he met the director of that very influential review, Jean Paulhan, who agreed to read his manuscript. Soon Roger received a long letter accepting the text on condition that he make certain changes, especially towards the end. He replied that he had conceived the work in its present form, as an expression of his own experience, and that any change in the conclusions would be false. This seems to have decided him against a literary career and he began to study theology at Lausanne.

In the summer of 1937 his first year of study was over and the doubts had returned. Was this really the way for him? Should he continue? Yet what reasons could he give for not going on? The end of the summer was near and registrations for the second year had to be submitted soon or not at all. What happened then was one of those events which often mark our entire future destiny. Lily, one of his married sisters, was due to give birth and she had fallen gravely ill. The issue seemed certain to be fatal. 'Then, perhaps for the first time ever, I really prayed. A very poor prayer! I simply said a Psalm to God. But it was a step forward.' Lily lived. For Roger it was like a miracle, an answer to his prayer. The immediate result was his registration for the second year of studies. As for the long-term consequences, who could say?

The second and third years were spent mainly at Lausanne, partly in Strasbourg. Before the start of the fourth and final year, Roger found himself invited to become the president of the Student Christian Federation. He had never had any contact with the people concerned and had never attended a meeting! In spite of a first refusal, the group would not take no for an answer. He soon sensed that the people involved in the movement were not always very solidly grounded in the dimension of prayer as search for God, nor in the sources of belief. He therefore proposed to organise a regular series of meetings all through the winter on those themes. It met with much more success than he had ever imagined.

By the summer of 1940 he was twenty-five, and needed only to write a short thesis for his studies to be complete. The idea of the next step was slowly taking shape; Roger was not able to prepare his future plans in quiet, abstract theories. The war had begun the autumn before, and for France it was already over. In 1941 Roger was to write: 'The defeat of France awoke powerful sympathy. If a house could be found there, of the kind we had dreamed of, it would offer a possible way of assisting some of those most discouraged, those deprived of a livelihood; and it could become a place of silence and work. . . .' That dream had grown during the twelve months prior to July 1940: a house to live in, to live the essential dimensions of the Gospel with others; a new reality, something not previously possible, because times change. Therefore, too, the choice of France, not Switzerland; the place must offer a space of freedom, be a country where people are open to new initiatives. So France it must be, a land of wartime suffering, but a land of inner freedom.

Into war, into life

August 1940 found Roger crossing into Vichy-controlled France. After the surrender of France the German armies had ceased their advance along a line that cut the country in two. Pétain and the government of unoccupied France were installed in the spa of Vichy. An uncle Marsauche was stationed as military chaplain at Bourg-en-Bresse, not far from Mâcon and Geneva. Roger's journey was ostensibly to pay him a visit, but nothing was to prevent him from looking at empty houses as well.

Scarcely an hour away from Geneva the dream already seemed to have found its fulfilment. A large house was available, not far from main roads and with a farm ready to support the new owner as soon as he moved in. Moreover, the house included a chapel where St François de Sales had celebrated Mass. The price would have been low, and Roger was tempted. Geneva was so close, though, and he decided to carry on farther into France, to see what other houses might appear. Near Bourg he found one, set in the lee of a hill, surrounded by high trees and with a wonderful view. Then he looked around and saw how prosperous everything was. Life here would be too easy, too comfortable! Other regions of France were poorer, and his father had always taught Roger that Christ is closest to the poor. So in mid-August we find Roger on his way to Cluny. Ruins do not interest him, but perhaps he felt that a wind of renewal had once swept through the Church because men had consecrated their lives to Christ in Cluny.

Walking through the narrow streets of the ancient town, Roger suddenly saw a paper fixed to a door: House for sale in Taizé. He knocked and was told that Taizé was a tiny village to the north, that the house in question had been empty for several years and he would find the keys with an old woman in the village. So the next morning he set off, cycling along the valley, with the river Grosne snaking through the fields to his right. Turning off the road and over the railway line, he found a rough cart-track leading up to the half-ruined village. In the village itself the road became bare rock. He found the old woman and together they visited the house. Then, since time was getting on, Roger asked where he would find something to eat. The old woman replied that he had best come and eat with her; there was no shop or café anywhere near. During the simple meal Roger told her something of his ideas. He had not been particularly struck by the house there, but all of a sudden he heard the old woman saying, 'Stay here with us; we are so poor, so isolated and the times are so bad!'

The decision still had to be made; it was not automatic. Roger returned to Switzerland and talked to friends, to his father. At the end of August he gathered some thirty friends at Lausanne to reflect on the idea. Out of that group was to evolve the first 'community' – not the brothers, but a network of friends who met regularly every two months, followed a common rule of life and were associated with Roger through those early years under the name of '*la communauté de Cluny*'. In early September Roger returned to Cluny and, rather to the attorney's astonishment, confirmed that he wanted to buy the house in Taizé. The old woman's words had made the difference. Roger could not know that at the same time the owners of the house, living destitute in Lyon, had decided to offer a novena (nine days of Mass and prayer) that their house might find a buyer. Madame de Brie, a woman of considerable piety, went to Mass for the ninth day of the novena and was back at the hospice where they had found refuge just in time to receive a telegram from Cluny. Their house had been sold to a young man from Switzerland. The author found this story hard to believe until Madame de Brie confirmed it for him. Until her death in 1977, she still came from time to time to visit the brothers at Taizé. She is now buried in the village churchyard, close to the house she once owned.

As soon as he arrived in Taizé, Roger saw that his first task was going to be a dangerous one. Only a few miles to the north lay the demarcation line. Above it, even more than in Vichy-administered France, people were on the run, hungry, hunted and in danger. At any hour of the day or night, Roger might see a refugee arriving at the gates of the house, sometimes half-dead from exhaustion. 'I never asked them who they were. I would let them into the house myself; I had to do everything. I had begun to clear and cultivate the land at once, milking the cow myself too. I set up a small chapel in the house where I would go to pray on my own. I dreaded the thought that some of the guests might feel obligated to pray with me out of a sense of gratitude. If they were not Christians, that would have been a kind of violence.' In fact, many of the refugees were Jews; from Taizé, they were passed on towards Switzerland and safety.

A common life alone? Roger knew that he had to wait. He could not force others to see things the same way as he did. The vocation to prayer and hospitality had to begin with him. Three times every day he withdrew to pray. The refugees kept on coming; sometimes there were a dozen in the house at once. There was constant danger, visits from the police. In November 1942 Roger was on his way back to Taizé from Switzerland, where he had been to gather money for his work with the refugees. At that time he was denounced to the authorities by somebody from the region. Even today Brother Roger's features express pain when he recalls the episode. He himself was warned in time, but on 11 November the house was occupied by the Gestapo and nobody knows what became of the refugees who were there at the time. Even though Roger and his sister Geneviève were exposed to very grave danger at that moment, he is careful never to imply any condemnation of those responsible. The cruelty of man for man, discovered by a person who admits that he was still very naive, was not seen as an excuse to give up. Roger continued in his vision, sure that every person is sacred, especially those in greatest need at any moment. How else can we interpret the sequel to these events, when Roger returned to Taizé after the war with his first brothers? He told this story in public for the first time at the Frankfurt Peace Prize ceremony: 'After the end of the war, there were German soldiers imprisoned in camps near Taizé. I obtained permission to have them brought over to our house for a service on Sunday mornings. That gave us a chance to share with them whatever food we had managed to find. It was a time of great shortage; we were all very poor. I soon noticed one of the prisoners in particular, he was so calm and radiant. He was a Catholic priest. In those days there was a backlash of hatred. One night, some women from the region whose husbands had perished in concentration camps in Germany broke into the camp and attacked the prisoners. It was an act of strange despair. By chance, their fury fell on that young priest, who was already in ill health. As a result he died. In his last hours he spoke only words of peace, love and forgiveness. In the course of the past months I had already realised that this young priest, this prisoner, was an image of God's holiness, in the fullest sense of the word.'

For Roger, the experience of those moments in 1942 when his life was in danger was an experience of fear; he admits it. Yet life continued, and since he was now obliged to be in Switzerland, he settled in a flat belonging to his family in Geneva. There, he returned to his unfinished studies, the thesis that had never been written. On 30 April 1943 he defended his work, a thesis entitled *The ideal of the monastic life before Saint Benedict and its conformity to the Gospels*. That topic, and the study of all the early monastic rules it entailed, was clearly not chosen by chance. However, the result was a piece of work for which today Brother Roger would not care to be remembered.

At almost the same moment, the door opened on two young men who had heard of Roger's ideas. In 1941 he had outlined some aspects of what a life in community might involve, and had them published in booklet form. Max Thurian was studying theology when he read those lines one day in a retreat house. Pierre Souverain, who came next, was studying agriculture at Zurich. Both were eager to join Roger in his spiritual adventure; their studies were clearly going to be of importance for what would follow. Soon the three, then four with Daniel de Montmollin, were living a common life in the Geneva flat. It was always full of other people as well: friends of past years, new friends, workers, trade-unionists. In their exchanges, one major question was that of 'perseverance'. How was it that so many people set out full of enthusiasm and vision in some form of commitment, only to lose interest bit by bit and finally settle down to 'a quiet life'? In 1941 Roger had already written: 'We are isolated from one another, and that breeds discouragement. How can we break with our over-individualistic traditions? How can we make full use of the wealth of possibilities offered when people work together, and live together in community?'

Committed for life

The autumn of 1944 brought liberation to France. Roger immediately returned to Taizé; this time he was not alone. The first years after the war were harsh. The local population had never been very understanding, and the welcome the brothers offered to German prisoners was not designed to make their life any easier. Poverty was rife and the temptation to move elsewhere must have been a strong one. Yet austerity is not necessarily grim and there seems to have been much laughter in the young community. They had taken as their own a simple rule of life that Roger had found and which the Community of Cluny had adopted several years before:

> Throughout your day let work and rest
> be quickened by the Word of God.

> Keep inner silence in all things
>> and you will dwell in Christ.
> Be filled with the spirit of the Beatitudes:
>> joy, simplicity, mercy.

There was no other rule. Year by year they all renewed their promise to keep on living together. Every day they gathered to pray three times in the chapel at the top of the house. There was much to be done in the few fields they farmed, and little for them to live on. Yet others in the region were still worse off. After any war, there are numbers of children who are not wanted anywhere. In the villages around Taizé, there were dramatic situations where children were either orphaned or rejected by their family.

Gradually the brothers found themselves in charge of a group of such boys. A house in the village was rented and Geneviève Schutz came to settle in Taizé. For twenty boys she was to become '*Maman*'. Today they are all grown up, married and have families of their own.

In 1948 the first French brother, Robert, came to join the others. That same year, the little village church was made available for their common prayer by a *simultaneum*, a system found in parts of France under which the Catholic authorities agree to a church building being used at the same time for non-Catholic services. The village of Taizé was still marked by attitudes which can be found throughout the region around Cluny. The church was scarcely used; there was no parish priest; Mass might be celebrated once a year, or not at all. The French Revolution and the destruction of the great abbey church of Cluny only seem to have consecrated an already widespread rejection of or indifference to the faith. The brothers at Taizé were not suspected only (or mainly) because they were Protestants in a land of Catholicism, but because they were believers in a region of general disbelief. Since Brother Roger had come to Taizé, one Mass had been celebrated there; in 1941 the Abbé Couturier, a great pioneer of Christian unity, had come to visit him and had celebrated in the ancient, neglected building. So the brothers submitted a request to the bishop of the diocese of Autun to be able to pray in the church. The answer, when it arrived, came from another source. It was a positive one, signed by Angelo Giuseppe Roncalli, the future Pope John XXIII, then nuncio in Paris! The request had seemed so unusual to the bishop that he had passed it on to higher authority. The first service in the church at Taizé was celebrated on the eve of Pentecost 1948.

Already Robert, the first French brother, had opened the way to others. While he completed his medical studies prior to becoming the local doctor at Taizé, two others followed him. That made in all seven brothers who, on Easter Day 1949, committed themselves for life to Christ in the community. In the village church that morning there were few witnesses: one young man who was later to become Brother Alain, and a visitor from Geneva, an Englishman called Oliver Tomkins who was to return to Taizé for the inauguration of the Church of Reconciliation in 1962 as Anglican bishop of Bristol!

The form of promise used that day has remained virtually unchanged ever since, for all the brothers who have followed them in the commitment of their lives:

Will you, for love of Christ, consecrate yourself to him with all your being? – I will.

Will you henceforth fulfil your service of God within our community, in communion with your brothers? – I will.

Will you, renouncing all ownership, live with your brothers not only in community of material goods but also in community of spiritual goods, striving for openness of heart? – I will.

Will you, in order to be more available to serve with your

brothers, and in order to give yourself in undivided love to Christ, remain in celibacy? – I will.

Will you, so that we may be of one heart and one mind and so that the unity of our common service may be fully achieved, adopt the orientations of the community expressed by the servant of communion, bearing in mind that he is only a poor servant in the community? – I will.

Will you, always discerning Christ in your brothers, watch over them in good days and bad, in suffering and in joy? – I will.

How do you translate the '*Veux-tu?* . . . *Je le veux*'? 'I want to, really, with all my heart'? Those promises, committing the whole future of each brother, have to be seen as the expression of a deep desire for Christ, and the joy of his calling. This is made plain by pages which, in 1949, Brother Roger had given the brothers a few days before Easter: in them was expressed a vision of the essential of their vocation, employing almost nothing but a series of quotations from the Gospels. Those lines remain; they are to be found at the end of what later became the Rule of Taizé, and they are read each time a brother makes his 'profession', his life-commitment.

It is typical of the brothers that they did not find it necessary, or perhaps even conceivable, to begin with a rule of life. No: live first, write afterwards! A minimum of guidelines is necessary, of course, but only the strict minimum. It was clear to the brothers from the beginning that this involved a risk but gave more freedom. With the years, the number of brothers increased: ten, twenty, thirty . . . today there are perhaps eighty or more. The exact number is hard to determine; the brothers refuse to treat themselves as statistics. Slowly a fuller statement of the common vision became necessary. 'What are we together for?' During the winter of 1952–53, Brother Roger withdrew into silence and in his retreat wrote out the Rule of Taizé. Nothing in it expresses obligation, it never employs 'you must'. You will not find it laying down any details about the timetable, or what the brothers should wear. The Rule is a common source for people committed in their inalienable freedom, as creators in common. In recent years, even the word 'Rule' has appeared too constricting to Brother Roger, and the most recent editions in French include other texts he has written and simply bear the title '*Les sources de Taizé*', an expression hard to translate into English but clearly implying that it has more to do with a spiritual vision of community life, with roots continually to be rediscovered, than with a legalistic document.

The text is worth reading, but remember that it will not describe Taizé to you, any more than you will be able to imagine the services there simply by reading an order of worship. The community for which the Rule was written consists of very real men, from some twenty different countries and from several different religious traditions. Each has his own odyssey which brought him one day to Taizé. Above all, each has his own gifts; the Rule was written to help stimulate each to give of his best, to create in common with all his brothers the 'parable of community' that Taizé is called to be in the Church and the world today. Freely, without constraint, for love of Christ and the brothers.

A parable of community

When news of the life-commitments of the first seven brothers became public, questions arose which, in one form or another, are always to be found about Taizé: Just what are these men? Are they Catholics or Protestants? Are they trying to start a new church, a new religious order? How is it possible for them to live together in this way? Finding answers to these questions is not made any easier by the fact that the brothers refuse to define themselves by other people's hard-and-fast categories, especially when they attempt to understand groups or individuals by setting them in opposition to other groups. 'If you're not *this*, you must be *that*. . . .' So often the very questions we ask determine to a great extent the responses we get, when perhaps the truest response would be to allow ourselves and our own mental categories to be called into question.

In the text read when a brother of Taizé makes his life-commitment, there is a phrase that helps us to understand better the community's vocation: 'The Lord Christ, in his compassion and his love for you, has chosen you to be in the Church a sign of brotherly love. It is his will that with your brothers you live *the parable of community*.' The word 'parable' calls to mind the New Testament, the stories told by Jesus to communicate his message. The details of the parables matter little in themselves; they are only important as part of a whole that helps us grasp something of the Gospel. Parables should not draw attention to themselves; they should point beyond themselves to reveal something of the living God.

Taizé has no pretensions to being an example or model for others to follow. The community wants to be a 'parable' that makes the Gospel call to reconciliation a reality, a tiny sign that helps people reflect on their own lives. Today, in front of the church at Taizé, the following sign is written in many languages: 'You who enter here, be reconciled and discover in the Gospel the spirit of the Beatitudes: joy, simplicity and mercy.'

The parable of community that Brother Roger has tried to live out with his brothers was confronted from the start with a Church divided into a host of different denominations, so it was natural for them to work for reconciliation in this area. Not that they saw reconciliation among Christians as an end in itself: what matters for Brother Roger is that the Church be a leaven of community and peace in the entire human family. But he has always been convinced that there will never be a lasting renewal of the Church, and the Church will never fully accomplish its mission, unless Christians are visibly reconciled among themselves.

In this sense, by its life the community asks a simple question: how can Christians witness to a God of love if they are divided? And the basic intuition which led to the existence of Taizé can perhaps be expressed in this way: 'It is true that we cannot solve, here and now, all the theological and other problems that have separated Christians throughout the centuries. But how can we remain passive when we hear the last words Jesus spoke concerning his disciples in John's Gospel: "may they be one so the world can believe"? And when we know that our divisions veil the face of God for so many people thirsting for Eternity's love? What we *can* do is begin with a concrete act, by sharing all we can share, and above all our lives. This concrete sharing of our lives will lead us to other steps.'

And in fact, year after year, new steps have been taken one after the other, not in response to a conscious strategy or a pre-set plan but to a desire to listen together to the Holy Spirit.

In the early years, the parable of community was limited but already significant: men from Protestant traditions where monastic life was unknown committed themselves for life in a monastic vocation. Without repudiating their background, they thus looked beyond the Churches of the Reformation and saw themselves as part of the wider monastic family. Yet even then, Brother Roger's intention was never merely to be part of a process of 'restoring' the monastic life within Protestantism; for him that would simply have consolidated the development of the different Christian bodies along parallel lines that never meet.

Perhaps he was strengthened in this resolve by a visit he made to England in 1946. There he saw the monastic communities which had come into being in the Church of England during the past hundred years or so, communities which were strictly 'Anglican' and whose existence, intentionally or not, simply strengthened the 'apartness' of the denomination to which they so explicitly belonged. Roger was looking for something quite different; to live out, in the lives of a few men, a parable of reconciliation that would put into the dough of the divided churches a leaven of communion. There could be no question of making Taizé into a 'Protestant concern' to be set up in parallel with similar Catholic or Orthodox institutions.

Reformed and Lutheran brothers were mingled in the community from quite early days. By the 1960s there were brothers from the Anglican Communion as well. There is no break with his origins when a person becomes a brother of Taizé, just as each brother is encouraged to be full of affection for his parents, whether father or mother understands his vocation or not. The community is not a new church. Then, in 1969, a further decisive step was taken in making the parable even more universal: a young Belgian doctor became the first Roman Catholic to enter the community. The president of the French Bishop's Conference was in full agreement with this step.

The arrival of Catholic brothers obliged the community to deepen its understanding of the 'parable of community' it was trying to live. During its annual council-meeting in 1969, the community worked out a text of which one section reads: 'The simple fact of having Catholic brothers among us stimulates us to live more and more in anticipation of unity by placing ourselves in communion with that minister who is the servant of the servants of God.' Already in preceding years, Brother Roger had occasionally expressed himself on the ministry of the Pope, and in the years to come he was to do so even more. Speaking in New York in 1971 to the bishops of the Episcopal Church (Anglican Communion), he said: 'We are contemporaries of John XXIII, that great witness to Christ. Is it now still possible for us to envisage the unity of the Church without even touching on the question of the Bishop of Rome? And yet there is still a conspiracy of silence around his ministry of unity, even among certain Catholics.

'Every local community needs a pastor, to gather together the flock always inclined to fragment and scatter. Can we really hope to see the Church gather in unity unless it has a similar pastor for its universality? Surely his vocation is to be at the very heart of the Church's life, not at the top of a pyramid, or acting as a kind of head (Christ is the head of the Church).

'Is the Bishop of Rome, as that universal pastor, already now drawing us closer to a Church of communion? If so, then he and his local Church will play a vital role in the promotion of worldwide unity.'

Clearly Brother Roger has thought much about these questions, and looked for ways for that 'anticipation of unity' to become a reality. He gave an even more precise expression of this during a European meeting of young adults held in Rome in 1980, in a public address in the presence of Pope John Paul II: '. . . without being a symbol of repudiation for anyone, I have found my own identity as a Christian by reconciling in myself the current of faith of my Protestant origins with the faith of the Catholic Church.' And in recent years, he has often spoken of the need for each Christian, while ecumenical agencies continue to search for a visible, institutional reconciliation, to achieve here and now a reconciliation within him- or herself by 'day after day, disposing ourselves inwardly to trust in the Mystery of Faith,' the Mystery of Faith in its entirety, and not just those parts with which we happen to agree. So we

31

can see how any 'either-or' mentality is utterly foreign to the vision of the Taizé Community.

In recent years, the parable of community that Taizé has been living out has undergone another, unexpected widening. The first brothers were all from two or three European countries, whereas today there are brothers from some twenty countries in Western and Eastern Europe as well as of other continents. Having brothers from Asia, Africa and America has made a great difference in the outlook of the community. Living and praying together from such different backgrounds is a small but very real sign of reconciliation in the human family as a whole, and that has been Taizé's passionate concern from the very start.

On the Move

WE HAVE seen the community become a reality. Perhaps it was inevitable that there should be incomprehension: the brothers knew that the novelty of their enterprise demanded risks that would not always be easy to understand from the outside. Now they had a life to live, important calls to respond to. Taizé is in a poor region; it may look attractive, but the soil is shallow and the farms are mostly too small to offer a real future. And life for the brothers could not be restricted to rural France. Modern man is very much the city-dweller at home with industry and technology. How were they to share this reality? In 1951, as soon as there were twelve brothers, two went to live and work in the mining area thirty miles north of Taizé, at Montceau-les-Mines. They were the first 'fraternity'; the Rule was soon to state that the brothers, wherever they went, were called to be 'signs of Christ's presence and bearers of joy'.

Across the earth

From that moment, Taizé was always to be partly 'abroad', with small groups of brothers forming 'fraternities' first in various parts of Europe, then later across the world. The fraternities can last a few months or a few years. They have been numerous at certain periods, limited at others when life on the hill itself demanded more of the community's energies. Some of them have been at the heart of dramatic tensions, particularly in Algeria during the war for independence, when the brothers were the only Europeans allowed to live among the Arabs. Others lived for five years in one of

Chicago's ghetto areas, among increasing racial tensions. For several years, brothers lived close to Dom Helder Camara in Recife (Brazil). In past years there have been fraternities of Taizé in such places as Kigali (Rwanda), Santiago (Chile), Sheffield (England), Abidjan (Ivory Coast), Utrecht (Holland), Cologne (Germany), San Antonio (Texas), Tokyo (Japan) and Hong Kong. In Calcutta, brothers of Taizé have twice spent six months working with Mother Teresa's Brothers of Charity, and since the meeting in Madras relations with the Indian subcontinent have grown even deeper.

Today there are fraternities on every continent, normally in a place marked by poverty or division. In going to the Southern hemisphere, the brothers do not see themselves as 'experts' who bring ready-made solutions from Europe; they go above all to share the life of the people. And this means first of all listening, especially in situations where mistrust and suspicion reigns, in order to allow trust to spring up.

Just as in Taizé, the common prayer is the centre of life in the fraternities. Three times each day, whether in a bamboo hut, a tin-and-cardboard shack or on the fifth floor of a tenement in the heart of a large city, the brothers come together for prayer. The singing of the brothers and their guests compete with transistor radios and the noise of traffic; the neighbours hear the prayer, and sometimes come to take part. The reserved Sacrament is placed in the brothers' tiny chapel, and silent prayer before the Eucharist is an important source of strength in such surroundings. In Kenya, where the brothers lived for seven years in Mathare Valley, one of the worst slums of Africa, their shack was often invaded by children who were happy to pray with the brothers and who understood intuitively the meaning of such a 'useless' presence. Guests are often welcomed for a simple meal with a time of silence, and this sharing of food extends the spiritual sharing of the common prayer.

The fraternities are also places of hospitality. Sometimes, as in Alagoinhas, in the North-East of Brazil, the brothers are able to welcome visitors for a few days of retreat, silence and sharing, as in Taizé. More often, the lack of space and the location of the fraternity makes this impossible, and people come instead for simple visits, for prayer or a meal.

Links between two fraternities situated in countries traditionally hostile to one another can lead to striking signs of reconciliation. This has been true for the brothers living in Japan and South Korea where, because of past history, friendship is rare between the two populations. In spite of this, at the intercontinental meeting in Madras, Koreans and Japanese were together, at the invitation of Taizé. At that meeting the same was true for Tamils and Singhalese living in Sri Lanka, where these two groups are at war with one another. Because of the brothers many relationships have been created between Japan and Bangladesh, where brothers have lived for many years, giving young people from a rich country like Japan the chance to discover a quite different reality and to begin a sharing.

Brothers living on other continents attempt to be active in the local Church and where possible take part in pastoral work. For the brothers in Nairobi, Kenya, the international Eucharistic congress offered a marvellous possibility to bring together the inhabitants of Mathare Valley and the Christian community as a whole, during a pilgrimage of the Cross they helped organise in the slum as part of the congress. Elsewhere, for part of the year brothers of a fraternity take to the road as pilgrims. This has been the case in New York City, where since 1978 brothers have been living in 'Hell's Kitchen', a changing neighbourhood with many Hispanics from Central America and the

Caribbean. As part of the 'worldwide pilgrimage of trust', they have undertaken pilgrimages to over sixty cities in the United States and Canada from Texas to Alaska, from California to the Gaspé Peninsula, invited by groups of churches for evenings and weekends of prayer, reflection and the discovery of people and places of hope in the local situation.

Signs of a coming spring

In the same spirit as the fraternities, the brothers have always made shorter visits; there are few parts of the world they have not seen. For years, Brother Roger himself has spent part of each year living in a Southern continent among the deprived and forgotten, as well as going to visit Church leaders to search with them for concrete signs of reconciliation. This 'pilgrim ministry' is an essential part of the vocation of Taizé.

Of all these visits and fraternities, one city has certainly received more than any other – Rome. The first visits came long before John XXIII, and in a very different atmosphere. In June 1948, the then Holy Office published a text more or less forbidding Catholics to have ecumenical contact and fellowship with other Christians. The brothers felt called to try and improve this situation. Cardinal Gerlier of Lyon, who was later to pave their way to John XXIII, obtained an audience for them with Pope Pius XII. During this first stay in Rome, in 1949, the brothers met various other personalities in addition to the Pope. Some were very reticent, while others were confident that better days must come. One friend during that first visit was Msgr Montini, later to become Pope Paul VI. Their efforts may have helped in the publication of another text by the Holy Office the following year, in which local bishops were given the responsibility of deciding when ecumenical activities could include Catholic participants.

Today, it is sometimes hard to realise the attitudes Christians felt towards one another at that time. The 'frozen winter of ecumenism' was still to last long years, and perhaps know even fiercer squalls before there would be any signs of a 'springtime of the Church'. In 1950 the brothers set out for Rome a second time; this visit is little known, yet it had its importance. 1950 was a Holy Year, and it was generally thought that Pope Pius would mark it by a solemn and infallible proclamation of the dogma of the Assumption of Mary. The language and piety of Marian devotion at that time were still very influenced by Mediterranean Europe – where much has changed since – and clearly the Protestant Churches of Northern Europe or elsewhere would have little sympathy for that. For Taizé, however, that was not so much the problem; nor was Brother Roger concerned, as he journeyed towards Rome for the second time, to oppose the conviction expressed in the dogma. What prompted him to take the step was the fact that since the proclamation of papal infallibility in 1870, it had never actually been invoked in practice. If now the Pope made use of the 1870 definitions in proclaiming a dogma, could the goal of unity between Catholic and non-Catholic Christians remain possible for the foreseeable future? The brothers went to Rome longing to be understood: if only Mary could be honoured in a way that would not close doors! If only the doors of unity could be kept open! They found friendship and understanding in some circles. But it is perhaps not surprising that for Pius XII such language was not convincing. The climate in the Catholic Church at that time was unprepared. So the Assumption was proclaimed in the expected style, and for Taizé, where the brothers had tried to arouse people's awareness to the hope of Christian unity, the backlash was cruel. 'In 1950 we realised that the confidence of many friends was going to evaporate. Our hope for a restored unity among all Christians began to lose interest for them.' The brothers never told of the efforts they had made, realising that to win sympathy in this way would give the lie to their vocation, since the road to unity could never involve coming together in opposition to another tendency or group. In the Church, reconciliation is not achieved by a crusade against others. In 1952, 1954 and 1955 they were invited to ecumenical talks in Rome. The results were minimal. The winter continued.

Then came 1958 and the election of Pope John. Brother Roger has written, 'Within an institution, however rigid it may be, if a single person arises who truly manifests the presence of Christ, then nothing, no barriers, can stand in the way of the outburst of charity.' With John XXIII, audiences with the founder of Taizé became yearly events; even before the announcement of the Council, a change had begun, some 'fresh air' began to circulate and some of the intolerable harshness of Christians towards other Christians began to vanish. At Taizé, the community was ready to take up the challenge when, on 25 January 1959, Pope John announced the Council.

In the summer of 1962, Brother Roger received a letter from Rome, from Cardinal Bea of the newly-created Secretariat for Christian Unity: 'For years past you have been active in ecumenical work, you have shown much interest in the activities of the Secretariat for Christian Unity, with which you maintain a cordial relationship. So this offers me the occasion of inviting you and the Revd Max Thurian to be present at the Second Ecumenical Vatican Council as observers, qualified as "guests of the Secretariat". . . . I am sure that with the help of the Holy Spirit, your presence at the Second Vatican Council will strengthen the bonds between all who not only confess Christ as Lord but labour for the great cause of unity.' So it was that when the Vatican Council was opened on 10 October 1962, many who saw the ceremony on television were struck by the two young men robed in white standing in a tribune with the other observers. What is not always realised is that the brothers were always there, every day at every moment of every session from the opening prayers until the end. Perhaps few of the Council Fathers could say as much!

'To be signs of Christ's presence and bearers of joy' is the task of the brothers in fraternity. The fraternity in Rome during the Council, in a small flat near the Forum, strove to be just that. In trying to ascertain the influential personalities at the Council, historians normally think of the great speeches, the moderators, the cardinals; but the meal-table of the Taizé fraternity should also be taken into account: 'When the morning assembly of the Council was over, we would go towards those we knew best and exchange our immediate concerns. . . . Then we had to find the bishops we had invited to come back home with us for the noon meal. The conversations at table, and the fact of sharing a common meal . . . offer us a foretaste of what we shall receive on the day visible unity comes about, in a single common Eucharist. . . . The food is simple, the meal is often full of laughter. Very often we end by going to the little oratory where we pray together in silence and say the Our Father. When everybody has left, we have a few moments to rest and relax; then all kinds of people start arriving to talk with us. Five of us are needed to welcome them all. Later, in the evening, we pray the Office and then it is time to welcome other guests, those invited for the evening meal. At the same time, we have to work on the Council debates, follow the evolution of the texts, write notes and expose our point of view when it is asked for.'

Brother Roger estimates that during the fourth session alone almost five hundred people came to share a meal with the brothers: observers, lay-auditors, bishops and cardinals!

One region of the world was particularly well-represented at those meals: Taizé had begun its close friendship with Latin America. Concern at European ignorance about, and indifference to, the evolutions taking place in that part of the world began to appear in Brother Roger's words and writings from 1958 onwards. This may seem surprising: why talk of other people's problems when for the first time there is a chance of talking about Christian unity in France and Europe? Because there the future could be found – a future of humanity, and the future of the Church. So many Christians on that continent, and such a high birth-rate: what role will the Church play in the future? And are we with them? Not a question of 'aid' or 'problems' but of 'hope for the future' and 'communion'.

Deep friendships grew up between Taizé and bishops from that continent. Some of them are well known: Dom Helder Camara of Recife, for example. In one of his journals Brother Roger relates the frequent visits of Dom Helder to the flat in Rome during the Council, where he would read out the speeches he was preparing. Cardinal Silva Henriquez of Chile, Dom Antonio Fragoso of Brazil. . . . . One of them did not live long enough, and that is one of the tragedies of our time: Manuel Larrain was one of the greatest bishops Latin America ever bestowed upon itself. Bishop of Talca (Chile), he was a co-founder and first president of CELAM, the Catholic Bishops' Conference of Latin America. For Brother Roger he was a close friend. One day, the story goes, Bishop Larrain was expected by one of the high dignitaries of the Roman Curia, and was afraid he would not be able to communicate what he wanted to say. Knowing that the person in question esteemed Taizé, he asked Brother Roger to go in his stead, and he spent the time of the meeing praying in a church nearby!

Later he was called away from Rome to be with his mother in her dying moments. Not having had time to say farewell to Brother Roger, at the airport he suddenly drew off his bishop's ring and sent it to him as a token of friendship. In 1966 Manuel Larrain was killed in a car accident. His ring remained in Taizé until 1974. Then, during his visit to Chile, Brother Roger gave it to Bishop Larraine's successor.

The clearest effect on Taizé of this friendship with Bishop Larrain was his role in stimulating 'Operation Hope'. Talca, like most dioceses, had lands which had become their property in various ways, often by bequest. Bishop Larrain decided to give the ownership of the land to the peasants working on it by creating co-operatives. Another Chilean bishop was working to create co-operatives among fishermen. Taizé agreed to help these initiatives by an ecumenical appeal for funds. The aim of 'Operation Hope' was 'to help finance initiatives taken by Latin Americans themselves, with a view to restoring a hope in life to people who have lost all hope.' Operation Hope also published an ecumenical version of the New Testament in South American Spanish, one million copies of which were distributed free of charge to the different Churches of Latin America. Later, half a million New Testaments in Portuguese were sent to Brazil.

Brother Roger continued his friendship with Latin America by attending both general assemblies of CELAM. In 1968 he was the personal guest of Pope Paul VI, travelling with him to Medellin (Columbia), and in 1979 he attended the meeting in Puebla (Mexico). At that meeting, the bishops' call for a 'preferential option for the poor and the young' cannot have failed to gladden his heart.

Pilgrims and friends

The community has not only been associated with creating co-operatives in far-off countries. At Taizé, in 1954, the brothers were contacted by a group of local farmers anxious about the future of their milk production. The factory which had until then collected their milk each day was threatening to stop doing so, in an attempt to lower prices. One brother, Alain, had studied agriculture and got together with the farmers. They agreed that the only possible long-term solution was to found a milk co-operative for the region. This they did, in spite of considerable opposition from vested interests, and soon it was collecting the milk from some twelve hundred producers. Later, in 1961, Pope John published the encyclical *Mater et Magistra* in which he spoke of socialisation, calling rural Christians to look for ways of socialising their activities. As a result the brothers decided with five local families to take the risk of founding a total farming co-operative. After a year of reflection, in September 1962, the COPEX came into being. There all work is done in common, with no consideration as to whose the fields are. In 1964 the brothers decided, as a sign of solidarity, to give to the COPEX all the fields they owned. Only the land on which the house stood remained apart.

As the 1960s began, not only did the brothers continue to travel to search for ways of reconciliation, but the numbers of visitors coming to the hill of Taizé began slowly to increase. The community, with the agreement of the Holy Office, organised a series of meetings bringing together Protestant pastors and Roman Catholic bishops. Also at this time, eight brothers went to England with Brother Roger, mainly to Sheffield where they found a good friend in the Anglican bishop, Leslie Hunter. From there they went to Canterbury. In 1962, Brother Roger spent a week with Patriarch Athenagoras in Istanbul: 'We shared his midday meal each day, talked freely together, sharing in his everyday life. . . . One day I told him, with some of the bishops who work with him also in the room, how John XXIII could not always do what he wanted; he replied, "In that case I love him more than ever!"'

42

Every year the number of visitors coming to Taizé to pray with the community was increasing; by this time, the little village church could not contain all the people present on certain Sundays. But how were they to build a more spacious church? No funds were available for such a project. Then one day a German organisation sent representatives to Taizé. *Sühnezeichen* (signs of reconciliation) had been set up by German Christians to construct signs of healing in regions which had been terrorised during the war. They organised both the fund-raising and the work-force of young volunteers. When they came to Taizé, they already had a long list of completed projects: hospitals, churches, synagogues and centres in various parts of the world. Taizé was a place of reconciliation, and Sühnezeichen would be prepared to take charge of the building of a church there. So in early 1961, the first group of fifty young volunteers arrived and after eighteen months, in the fields outside the village, a church was ready for use. Built on plans prepared by Brother Denis, an architect, the Church of Reconciliation was inaugurated by an ecumenical celebration on the Feast of the Transfiguration, 6 August 1962.

The list of friendships and visits to the hill in Burgundy since those days is far too long to be mentioned here. But one person has to be named, since he played such an important role in bringing the community out of its long 'winter'. Eugene Carson Blake was named as General Secretary of the World Council of Churches at Geneva in 1966; at once, even before taking up his post, he came to Taizé on a first visit. He expressed interest and appreciation for the ecumenical work of the community. That was very new and very warming, after the previous complaints by some of the leading figures of the WCC that Taizé did not represent anybody and had no right to do what it was doing. In his six years in office, Dr Carson Blake was a frequent visitor to Taizé. In July 1968, he invited Brother Roger to address the

WCC Assembly at Uppsala (Sweden). Brother Roger spoke at the very beginning of the assembly, as soon as the official speeches were over. Other brothers were with him, and also played a role in the life of the assembly. The following year the community was invited to take part in the work of SODEPAX, an organisation set up to allow the Vatican and the WCC to make joint efforts in the fields of justice and peace. Brother Christophe was sent by the community to take up this work, and he continued in Geneva until his untimely death in 1973. A few years later, Brother Max would play a similar role in Faith and Order, an effort of collaboration between Catholic and Protestant theologians to discover the common roots of their faith.

The WCC held its next assembly in 1975 in Nairobi (Kenya). This was the first time it had been held in Africa. Brothers from Taizé were again present. Along with a group of four young people – two Europeans, one boy from Indonesia and another from Cameroon – they lived in two simple homes in a poor district of the city, far from the European-style hotels. The brothers were the guests of a young Muslim who shared his home with them. Every evening delegates were invited out to visit them. Evening prayers, silence, then a simple meal involved delegates and Nairobi inhabitants in a few hours of sharing which were otherwise rare during those busy days. A bishop from Russia confirmed this when he told the little fraternity, 'Here you represent the Pilgrim'. The next WCC General Assembly was in Vancouver (Canada), on the other side of the earth, and Brother Roger and his brothers were present there too.

Among the many other visits worth mentioning are those to Taizé in 1973 of the then Archbishop of Canterbury, Dr Michael Ramsey, and in 1984 of his successor, Dr Robert Runcie. In August 1976 and in October 1983, Mother Teresa of Calcutta came to Taizé for days of prayer and

Three-year-old Roger out walking with an aunt and one of his sisters (*photo: Taizé*)

The village of Taizé (*photo:Stein*)

A familiar sight, the hill crowded with young people: in the background, the Church of Reconciliation with a circus-tent attached in order to accommodate everyone (*photo: Taizé*)

The Intercontinental Meetings in Taizé (*photos: all Taizé*)

A PILGRIMAGE OF
TRUST ON EARTH

PELLEGRINAGGIO DI
FIDUCIA SULLA TERRA

PELERINAGE DE
CONFIANCE SUR LA TERRE

EEN PELGRIMAGE VAN
VERTROUWEN OP AARDE

BARCELONA

MADRID

PEREGRINACIÓN DE CONFIANZA
A TRAVÉS DE LA TIERRA

PILGERWEG DES VERTRAUENS
AUF DER

Common prayer in the Church of Reconciliation (*photo: Taizé*)

Everyday, one of the brothers gives a Bible introduction to the young people (*photo: Taizé*)

Individual prayer is one of the aspects of life in Taizé (*photo: Taizé*)

Brothers live in small fraternities among the poor across the world. Here, in 'Hell's Kitchen', New York, one of the brothers with some young people from the neighbourhood (*photo: Brass*)

For years, one of the fraternities shared in the life of Mathare Valley, Nairobi, Kenya (*photo: Hans Lachmann*)

retreat. On two separate occasions, the community welcomed the Archbishop of Cracow, Cardinal Karol Wojtyla, before he was known to the world as Pope John Paul II. And there was that last encounter with Patriarch Athenagoras in Istanbul, with his dramatic farewell: lifting his hands as though holding a chalice, he cried to the departing brothers, 'The cup and the breaking of bread, remember, there is no other way!'

5 October 1986

This Sunday morning, Taizé is waiting for the visit of a very special pilgrim. Pope John Paul II has decided to stop by during his third trip to France. Seven thousand young people have arrived, most of them the night before, to join the brothers in welcoming the Pope. Those who could not fit into the Church of Reconciliation or in the large attached tent are gathered outside. Television screens will enable them to follow what is going on. During the entire night, a vigil of silent prayer has taken place in the village church.

At 8.30 am, the brothers leave the church to welcome the Pope. The entire region is covered with a thick fog. The helicopters could not leave their hangars and so the Pope has to come from Lyon in an ordinary car.

As he leaves the car and embraces Brother Roger, it is obvious that John Paul II feels at home with Taizé and its founder. As Archbishop of Cracow he had already visited Taizé twice, and had received Brother Roger both in Poland and, after being elected Pope, often in Rome.

In entering the Church of Reconciliation and greeting the young people who are singing while waiting for him, the Pope is reminded of the two European meetings that brought together some 25,000 young Europeans in Rome. He had joined them for prayer in Saint Peter's.

John Paul II takes his place on a small platform where

there is an armchair of wood and straw. Brother Roger, surrounded by children, speaks a few words of welcome:

'If the heart were to express all our gratitude and all our happiness in welcoming you to Taizé, it would take days and days.

'For decades now, the conscience of Christians has been awakened, perhaps as never before, to the urgent need for justice and peace. And now across the earth so many of the young, often with astonishment, are discovering in the Risen Christ the meaning of their lives. It is as if a longing for God has arisen when everything was covered with a thick cloud of indifference. As a result, it can be sensed that the coming century will be one of deep faith.

'This hope does not cause us to forget in particular those who are brought to a standstill by discouragements and by an attitude of "what's the use?". Some have been marked by broken relationships of all sorts, especially within families. Their hearts at times are dying of abandonment. Yes, human abandonments and loneliness are among the deepest wounds of our time. How then could we not devote all our energies to enable everyone to discover a source of communion?

'You know, most Holy Father, that week after week young Europeans come to Taizé to pray and to draw upon the sources of faith, while remaining attentive to the building up of the vast human family. The daily aspiration of my brothers and myself is for every young person to discover Christ, not Christ taken in isolation, but the "Christ of communion" present in fullness in that mystery of communion which is his Body, the Church. There many of the young can find a place to commit their whole lives to the very end, and to do so without a levelling of values. There they have all they need to become creators of trust, of reconciliation, not just among themselves but together with all the generations, from the very old to little children.

46

'In our community of Taizé, following the "Christ of communion" is like a fire that burns us. We would go to the ends of the earth to look for ways, to ask, to call, to implore if need be, but never from the outside, always while remaining within that unique communion which is the Church.

'Dear Holy Father, can I say to you in simplicity of heart that, attentive to your ministry as universal pastor, my brothers and I love you. Your coming to Taizé calls forth a joy that touches the depths of the soul.'

And now it is the Pope's turn to speak to the young. The words ring out in a strong Slavic accent, and have a significance that makes them well worth reprinting here in part:

'I thank you, dear Brother Roger, for the words full of trust and affection you have just addressed to me. And I greet you all in the joy of Christ. . . . Like you, pilgrims and friends of the community, the Pope is only passing through. But one passes through Taizé as one passes close to a spring of water. The traveller stops, quenches his thirst and continues on his way. The brothers of the community, you know, do not want to keep you. They want, in prayer and silence, to enable you to drink the living water promised by Christ, to know his joy, to discern his presence, to respond to his call, then to set out again to witness to his love and to serve your brothers and sisters in your parishes, your towns and villages, your schools, your universities, and in all your places of work. Blessed be Christ who, here in Taizé, and in many other places in his Church, causes springs of water to well up for the travellers thirsting for Him that we are!

'Today, in all the Churches and Christian communities and even among the highest political leaders in the world, the Taizé Community is known for the trust always full of hope that it places in the young. It is above all because I share this trust and this hope that I have come here this morning.

'Dear young people, to bring to the world the joyful news of the Gospel, the Church needs your enthusiasm and your generosity. You know, it can happen that your elders, after the difficult journey and the trials they have undergone, fall prey to fear or weariness and let the dynamism which is a mark of every Christian vocation grow weak. It can also happen that institutions, because of routine or the deficiencies of their members, are not sufficiently at the service of the Gospel message. Because of this the Church needs the witness of your hope and your zeal in order to fulfil her mission better. Do not be content to criticise passively or to wait for persons or institutions to become better. Go towards the parishes, the student organisations, the different movements and communities, and patiently bring them the force of your youth and the talents you have received. Bring your trust and support to the ministers of the Church; they are your servants in the name of Jesus, and for that reason you need them. The Church needs your presence and your participation. If you remain within the Church, you will of course at times be upset by divisions, internal tensions and the sad state of its members, but you will receive from Christ, who is the Head, his Word of Truth, his own Life, and the Breath of Love that will enable you to love him faithfully and to make your life a success by risking it in a joyful gift for others. . . .'

After finishing his talk, the Pope goes down among the brothers and kneels for a few minutes in their midst. He reads a prayer often used in Taizé: 'O God, we praise you for the multitudes of women, men, young people and children who, across the earth, strive to be witnesses of peace, trust and reconciliation. In the footsteps of the holy witnesses to Christ of every age, beginning with Mary and

48

the Apostles, enable us to dispose ourselves day after day to place our trust in the mystery of the faith of your Church, through Jesus Christ, your Son, our Lord.' Then, as the assembly continues to sing, the Pope goes downstairs into a small room to meet the brothers personally. He greets each of them individually, then speaks some words from the heart to the entire community. He leaves with them a written message that touches the brothers deeply. One of them told me afterwards that if you wanted to explain the community's vocation to someone, you could simply read them that message. They see it as an important confirmation of the life they have chosen:

'Dear Brothers, in the family-like intimacy of this brief meeting, I would like to express to you my affection and my trust with these simple words, with which Pope John XXIII, who loved you so much, greeted Brother Roger one day: "Ah, Taizé, that little springtime!"'

'My desire is that the Lord may keep you like a springtime that blossoms and that He keep you little, in the joy of the Gospel and the transparency of brotherly love. Each of you came here to live in the mercy of God and the community of his brothers. In consecrating your whole being to Christ for love of him, you have found both of these. But in addition, although you did not look for it, you have seen young people from everywhere come to you by the thousands, attracted by your prayer and your community life. How can we not think that these young people are the gift and the means the Lord gives you to stimulate you to remain together, in the joy and the freshness of your gift, as a springtime for all who are searching for true life? Throughout your days, work, rest, prayer, everything is quickened by the Word of God that takes hold of you, that keeps you little, in other words children of the heavenly Father, brothers and servants of all in the joy of the Beatitudes.

'I do not forget that in its unique, original and in a certain sense provisional vocation, your community can awaken astonishment and encounter incomprehension and suspicion. But because of your passion for the reconciliation of all Christians in a full communion, because of your love for the Church, you will be able to continue, I am sure, to be open to the will of the Lord. By listening to the criticisms or suggestions of Christians of different Churches and Christian communities and keeping what is good, by remaining in dialogue with all but not hesitating to express your expectations and your projects, you will not disappoint the young, and you will be instrumental in assuring that the effort desired by Christ never slackens to recover the visible unity of his Body, in the full communion of one and the same faith. You know how much I personally consider ecumenism a necessity incumbent upon me, a pastoral priority in my ministry for which I count on your prayer.

'By desiring to be yourselves a "parable of community", you will help all whom you meet to be faithful to their church affiliation, the fruit of their education and their choice in conscience, but also to enter more and more deeply into the mystery of communion that the Church is in God's plan. By his Gift to his Church, Christ liberates in every Christian forces of love and gives them a universal heart to be creators of justice and peace, able to unite to their contemplation a struggle along the lines of the Gospel for the integral liberation of human beings, of every human being and of the entire human being.

'Dear Brothers, I thank you for having invited me and thus having given me the opportunity to return to Taizé. May the Lord bless you and keep you in his peace and his love!'

It is time to go. John Paul II approaches his car, then suddenly decides to go back to the church to take his leave of the young people. 'I have to tell you that I am leaving,' he says. 'And with sadness. But the Pope must obey. He has many superiors!' A peal of laughter rings out, quickly followed by applause, and the singing begins once again, as the Pope sets off.

Taizé and the Young

PATRICK IS a young French doctor who decided to work among the poor of Colombia. Recently on a visit to Europe, he recounted something that had happened to him in Latin America:

'One day I went to visit a monastery located in the depths of the jungle, several hours on foot from the nearest town. I was warmly welcomed by the monks. I told one of them how it happened that I had decided to work among the poor: it was on account of a community in my home country, France. I had been going there for ten years, and finally I was led to take a further step. Without Taizé, I told him, I would not be here today, speaking with you. The Colombian monk replied with a smile: Neither would I be here if I had not been to Taizé; that's where I discovered my vocation!'

How is it that a small monastic community in an out-of-the-way French village has affected the lives of so many people across the globe? Why are so many of the young in particular attracted to Taizé, and what do they find there? Of course these questions are too vast to find the answers in any book, but perhaps in telling the story of the community's growing relationship with its young visitors, and especially by letting some of these visitors speak for themselves, we can allow a portrait to emerge, or rather a few snapshots of a reality that is still very much in the process of becoming.

A place where people pray

Taizé is a place people visit. That was not planned. The people coming there are from a host of different countries and continents, belong to different Church traditions, are of other religions, profess no belief, could not express what they believe. They are young, they are adults, they are old. They are workers, they are students, they are unemployed. They come to deepen their faith, to learn to pray, to meet other people, because they want to find out more. What do they find at Taizé?

Since 1962, they find the Church of Reconciliation. It is always open and there is the invitation to enter, whoever you are, to respect the silence and to share in the prayerful worship celebrated there. The building itself is a typical example of the application of the provisional. Once the floor was of bare concrete slabs, now it is covered with cheap carpeting. There are no pews. Nothing separates the brothers from the guests praying with them except an icon and a straggling line of green branches. Until 1971, the church had solid walls giving on to the level ground to the west. In that year, seeing that many of those coming for Easter would not find room inside the church, the community decided that welcome was more important than walls. The walls were demolished and a tent erected. The forms of prayer too change and evolve. Once only French was used, now the prayers and readings are always in a great variety of languages.

Three times each day, the bells ring out. The discussion groups stop talking, the 'welcome' closes down, the kitchen team leaves its pots and puts down its knives. Everyone, brothers and pilgrims, stops their activity and heads towards the Church of Reconciliation. Whether you are at Taizé for a week, a month, or for life, everything is centred on prayer.

For the new arrivals, it can be surprising or even frightening to discover that you are expected to attend prayer three times in a single day. 'At home I go regularly to church on Sunday,' one boy from Sweden told me, 'but I was rather apprehensive at the thought of going to church so many times in one week.' And what about those who never go to church at home! In fact, by the end of the week the question is usually turned around: 'How can we continue in our daily lives what we have discovered here?' And not a few discover prayer as a vital need. Valerie: 'When I went into the church for the first time something deep in me was touched. I never knew that a prayer of that sort existed. It took hold of me, almost violently. For the first few days, I felt I was being carried by the prayer of the others. Then, by the end of the week, I was praying myself.'

When you enter the Church of Reconciliation, the first thing that strikes you is the silence, the atmosphere of quiet peace. Candles flicker in the dim light, illuminating icons that welcome you and help you to enter into the mystery of God. The Virgin Mary, holding the Child Jesus and offering him to the world; Jesus with his arm round the shoulders of his friend; the Trinity, also known as the Icon of Hospitality; and in a central position, the icon of Jesus on the cross, arms outstretched to embrace all humanity.

At the front, the altar is in the centre. Behind it, a host of tiny candles placed in box-like depressions made of bricks. Everything is simple and beautiful. The red light that indicates the reserved Sacrament catches your eye. This silence is inhabited by the Risen Christ, present in the Eucharist.

The church is open day and night. At any hour you can find young people at prayer, sitting or kneeling on the floor. Some are bowed low, their foreheads touching the ground, in an age-old posture that symbolises the gift of one's entire being to God.

'Here I discovered,' said Rachel from England, 'that prayer is not only saying words to God; it is also listening. It is consenting to remain in God's presence even when nothing seems to be happening.'

During the times of common prayer, the brothers are in the centre of the church surrounded by all the visitors. They wear white robes, a sign that their whole being has been clothed by Christ, an expression of their identity as a community and a means of praising God other than by words.

In their desire to welcome others, the brothers have always looked for a liturgy that is accessible to all. Prayer in Taizé is inspired by the great monastic tradition: the chanting of Psalms, Scripture readings, intercessions, prayers read out. The diversity of languages used is more inhabitual: English, German, Swedish, Spanish, Italian, Portuguese, French, Polish, Korean, Chinese, Japanese, etc. It is important that each person present can hear something in his or her own language, even if only a single Bible verse. Reading the Gospel in ten different languages is a kind of parable of unity in diversity; it gives one a sense of the universality of the Church.

In this liturgy, the music is another distinctive feature. The community wanted to allow everyone to participate in the singing: how to do this given the great diversity of languages and the fact that many people stay only a few days and have no time to learn complex pieces? The solution found was brand-new and yet, although the brothers only realised this fully later on, had roots in an age-old tradition: refrains composed of a few words from Scripture were set to music and sung as a canon or ostinato. Throughout the centuries, a few words repeated over and over again have been an aid to contemplative prayer, building up little by little an inner unity of the person before God. For example, the 'Jesus prayer' in the Eastern Church, or the angel's greeting to Mary. These chants allow basic Gospel truths to penetrate us; the melodies remain alive within us long after we have left the church, as a kind of 'prayer without ceasing'.

In this way the songs of Taizé were born. Today they have been published throughout the world, and are used in many different places. I met a young Irish lad in Taizé who was astonished to find the community singing the songs . . . of his parish! They are well known in North America, and have been translated into Polish, Czech, Croatian, Hungarian. . . . You can hear them sung in Bengali in the slums of Calcutta, in Kiswahili in Nairobi, in Korean in Seoul, in Chinese in Hong Kong, in Spanish in Latin America. . . . In order to avoid giving too much room to French, the first chants were composed to Latin texts: '*Ubi caritas et amor, Deus ibi est*' ('Where charity and love are, God is there'), but today many different languages are used, and so the prayer is also a time to discover the beauty of languages other than one's own. In 1981, during the first European meeting organised by Taizé in London, St Paul's Cathedral, filled to overflowing, resounded with these chants. Many were in English. Two, however, were in German, and one older London dweller, who still remembered the Second World War bombings, wrote the following account:

'It was getting late one evening, and the steps of Saint Paul's were beginning to empty. As we descended the escalator of the Underground singing welled up from below: *Bleibet hier and wachet mit mir, wachet und betet* ('Stay here and keep watch with me, watch and pray'). Sudden lump in throat, as a childhood picture returned of another crowd, forty years ago, sheltering from the blitz on that very platform, and here are the children and grandchildren of our former enemy, singing that lovely song in a language I grew up to hate and am now beginning to love.'

A long time of silence after the Bible readings is at the

heart of every common prayer at Taizé. 'A time to reflect on the words that have just been read,' explained a German boy, 'a time of personal prayer, or simply a time to rest with others in God's presence. Perhaps that is when we become most aware of that Other who is within us.' Mornings and evenings, the silence is followed by a long litany that Brother Roger describes as a 'pillar of fire; there are intercessions for the Church, the world, the persecuted, those forgotten, those who suffer. . . . In the evening, the sung intentions are followed by spoken petitions for people in different countries. At the end of the evening prayer, many of the young people remain in the church and the singing continues, sometimes for hours. Some of the brothers in their white robes are there too, to help sustain the chants and to listen to those who have something personal they would like to confide. As the information sheet given to everyone who arrives in Taizé explains: 'To listen to you, if you want to speak about something that hurts you or which obstructs the paths of a search for the living God, some brothers remain in the church after the evening prayer; perhaps being listened to is a way for you to break through what is inhibiting you or to discover a path for your life.' The ministry of listening is very important in Taizé. For years now the Sisters of St Andrew have been participating in it, and week-long silent retreats often provide the occasion for young adults to discover a new direction for their life.

Although the brothers wish their prayer to be a space of beauty that 'opens us to the joy of God on earth', they are equally insistent that it not be divorced from the concerns of the world in which we live. 'Taizé is no super-pious place where religion is removed far from reality,' wrote Sue, a girl from Nottingham, England, who first came with a group of people to Taizé in 1981. 'It is a hard place to be because it demands decisions – maybe only little ones, the next step on your journey – but you come home a different person. A few layers of you are peeled off so that your centre is near the surface. Your inhibitions about praying are lost in the anonymity of the crowd. Here the norms are beauty and simplicity and openness and acceptance. It quickly becomes natural to go to church three times a day – to go in early and come out late. Worship ceases to be something unnatural and removed from life, but the thing that catches it all together and permeates everything. It is stressed that we must return to our own local communities and put into practice the insights we have gained. Far from being journey's end it is journey's beginning, but we are not lone travellers. We are accompanied by one another and by Christ.'

A call to commitment

If Taizé is a place where people pray, it is at the same time – and because of this – a place to discover the meaning of one's life in communion with many others. Mother Marie-Tarcisius, the elderly superior of the Sisters of Saint Andrew who live in the next village and who have worked closely with the brothers for over twenty years, sees this as one of the most important things that happens on the hill. 'The young people who come here receive a "shock of meaning",' she says. They see their own life with new eyes, as well as the role they are called to play in the Church and in society as a whole.

This is confirmed by the information sheet given to everyone as soon as they arrive in Taizé. It contains these words:

'As you arrive in Taizé, understand that it is part of the community's vocation to welcome you so that you can approach the living springs of God through prayer, through the silence of contemplation, through searching. . . . You have come to Taizé to find a meaning to your life. One of Christ's secrets is that he loved you first. There lies the meaning of your life: to be loved for ever, to be clothed by God's forgiveness and trust. In this way you will be able to take the risk of giving your life.'

Discovering in Christ's love for us the meaning of life, and as a result being drawn to take the risk of giving one's own life: although people come to Taizé for a host of different reasons, in the long run, this is undoubtedly why so many of them keep coming back. Week after week, the question of giving one's life, of commitment, is one of the most important topics in Taizé. The simple presence of the brothers is already a challenge to many. Anne from Marseille explains, 'When I took part in the prayer I was struck to see hundreds of young people in the church and, in the centre, the brothers, men of all ages and from different continents. In the past, I often wondered whether it was possible to say yes, how to find the strength, why to commit oneself to follow Christ. . . . It was important for me to see the community of brothers praying, to see these men who dare to remain faithful.'

The question of a life-commitment is a topic of reflection both in Taizé and in the meetings the brothers organise elsewhere in the world. How can we say yes to Christ for a lifetime? During the European meeting in Cologne, Germany, in 1984, this topic was one of the many possible choices for the 'workshops' one afternoon. More than a thousand participants chose to attend this particular group, crowding into the room where it was to be held, which had suddenly become far too small.

After a Bible introduction on the subject, the young people look for answers: how to respond to Christ by a definitive 'yes' in marriage or celibacy? But also, how does the decision to follow Christ affect one's studies, professional life, or the use of one's time? Group sharing is important to find answers to these questions, but so is silence, prayer and personal dialogue with a brother or a sister. The question of a life-commitment leads many of the young people to spend a week in silence.

A week in Taizé can also be an occasion to confront the hesitations and fears that can spring up when the question of commitment arises. In his letters, Brother Roger often deals with this question: 'When you begin to understand that this yes commits your entire life, you become aware of a great unknown: how can I ever hold true? First there is hesitation and a "no", in a startled reaction that is almost an integral part of our human condition' (*Letter from the Desert*). And he reminds us that no one is built naturally for living the Gospel. Faced with Christ's call to give everything, our first response is a prayer: 'Give me the gift of giving myself.' After spending a week in silence in Taizé, a young man wrote: 'I feel free. I understand now that following Christ does not mean marching behind someone as an obligation, as I had unconsciously imagined. Following him means remaining in his love, being called his friends, and bearing fruit.'

Those who spend a week in Taizé also discover that others, many others, from different cultures and situations are asking the same questions. How can we live the Gospel to the very end? They realise that others have already begun to reply and that the road is not just for a select few. Many people find that listening to the experiences of others gives them more courage. In the discussion groups, you often hear it said that it is important to take a small step to begin, and that these small steps will point the way to the gift of an entire life. Anne from Marseille put it this way: 'I discovered that with a tiny seed of faith you can say yes, you can set out knowing almost nothing, and succeed in something you could never even have imagined.'

Along the same lines Brother Roger has written: 'If a

trusting heart were at the beginning of everything, you would be ready to dare a "yes" for your whole life.' Trust. The word is essential, for Taizé reminds us that we are not the ones who have to accomplish everything. We respond to a call and, beyond our hesitations and our fears, we are astonished to discover that 'a yes has been placed by God's Spirit in our innermost being.'

'The young person in the Gospel began by saying no. God, who never imposes himself, did not force his lips. But the young person understood that this refusal caused an alienation within him. If he said no, he was no longer being consistent with what was inside him, the Spirit of God, who deep within him was saying yes, with the same yes that was in Mary. By letting this yes rise up from your depths, it is possible for you to say, "I will".

'A yes because of Christ leaves you vulnerable. It makes it impossible for you to run away from yourself and from an essential solidarity with others.' (*Letter from the Desert*)

To close this section, let us listen to two young people who explain how their visits to Taizé brought them closer to a commitment. Neville is from Leeds, in England:

'After my last visit to Taizé, I felt determined to understand and respond to the voice of those for whom life offers few choices. Whilst there is much around which can make us feel despondent and that there is little hope for something better, there is hope. This kind of hope does not lie in the politicians or church leaders alone, but among the people themselves, amongst those who welcome you into their homes for a cup of coffee, or simply to talk and share something of themselves with you. This hope draws its strength and "power" from the most vulnerable corners of society, a quiet undercurrent that flows through people's lives.

'Shortly after returning to Leeds from Taizé, I worked with a local church in setting up a small self-help project to respond to the needs and aspirations aroused by unemployment. I was unemployed myself last year, and together we worked in small ways to build a hope. Those with whom I was fortunate enough to work were Bengalis, Vietnamese and Pakistanis mainly. As you can see, there is more to the inner city than riots and robbery, there is the glimmer of possibilities as yet unrealised, and the presence of Christ who sustains.'

Michael is a young priest working in a busy parish in the South of England:

'Taizé turned my life upside down. I think I owe my vocation to the brothers there, though not everyone will find what I found. My whole experience of Christianity was enriched by the community life on the hill and the common prayer. The words were backed up by actions, in a way I had not discovered before. I'd been through some very difficult times, and it was, at that time, the only place I could go where I knew I would be listened to and understood. I was very conscious of being understood there. In the growth of spirituality, recognising what is my life in relation to Christ, the brothers understood what was going on within me, even to the point of recognising my vocation to the priesthood when I could not.'

Christ is risen!

Holy Week 1970. A group of young people from all the continents are gathered around Brother Roger in Taizé. In this group most are from the Southern continents, from peoples whose voice is rarely heard: so at Taizé it shall be heard. For seven months now, since the previous summer, everyone has been invited to take part in a search-process. At a time of widespread pessimism and sadness in both Church and world, what joyful news of hope can we announce today? What news is capable of restoring joy to the whole Church of Christ beyond its present disarray? The intercontinental team has been invited to read the results of the search undertaken during the winter, and try to discern the essential.

For the first time at Taizé, Easter is crowded. Almost no accommodation exists, the cold is bitter, yet 2,500 have come for the 'joyful news' promised. It is Easter, the news will be paschal, and the Resurrection is going to become the centre of what follows. But as they squeeze into the church that Easter afternoon, they do not know that yet. The members of the team begin to speak: 'Last year, we proposed that we should announce some "joyful news". So we have listened to suggestions made by young people of every continent. Concerned as we are that there be reciprocity between North and South, we have received the essential from the South. There, young Latin Americans have expressed "the urgent need for a Church more and more paschal, a Church that refuses all means of power, faithfully witnessing to a Gospel that sets people free". Young people in Africa and Asia see those of the Northern world stifling the values which are theirs – values of communion, of sharing and of festival.

'So the news we have to announce is paschal news:

'*The risen Christ comes to quicken a festival in the innermost heart of man.*

'*He is preparing for us a springtime of the Church, a Church devoid of means of power, ready to share with all, a place of visible communion for all humanity.*

'*He is going to give us enough imagination and courage to open up a way of reconciliation.*

'*He is going to prepare us to give our lives so that man be no longer victim of man.*'

These four lines, which would stimulate the young people's searching for years to come, were expanded and commented upon in the following text:

'We celebrate the Risen Christ in the Eucharist. By it we are given to share in the life of the Risen Christ and to participate in the paschal mystery: to share in the trials of Christ who, until the end of time, suffers in his Body, the Church, and in our brothers and sisters: to live at the deepest levels within ourselves the festival always offered by the Risen Christ, he who alone transfigures the depths of our being. The Eucharist is there for us who are weak and defenceless. We receive it in a spirit of poverty and in repentance of heart. In our journey through the desert towards a Church of sharing, the Eucharist gives us courage not to store up manna, to give up material reserves and to share not only the bread of life but also the goods of the earth.

'We celebrate the Risen Christ by our love for the Church, a love that kindles a fire on the earth. If the Church is in one way like an underground river which, in a hidden, secret movement, assures a continuity that flows from the very first Pentecost, it is also a "city set on a hill to be seen by all". By the visibility of our brotherly love, by our rediscovered unity, the Church is called to become an unparalleled ferment of fraternity, of communion, of sharing, for all humanity: that is the essence of its ecumenical vocation. On the eve of his death Christ prayed that our unity would make it possible for the world to believe.

'We celebrate the Risen Christ in our brothers and sisters. Living by prayer and by trust in one another – poor values – we discover that people are "sacred by the wounded innocence of their childhood, by the mystery of their poverty". In human beings we see the very face of Christ, "above all when tears and sufferings have made this face more transparent". So we will give even our life so that man be no longer victim of man.'

Easter Day 1970 marked the beginning of a new stage in Taizé's common journey with the young. Young people had begun visiting the community in the late 1950s, and so a centre of hospitality was opened in a neighbouring village. Soon this was found to be too far away, and slowly, thanks to the efforts of work-camps, simple accommodations began to rise on the hill itself. In early September 1966, the first large international youth meeting took place. Adults were invited too, including the aged Cardinal Bea. The brothers reckoned that the meeting would happen 'and that would be that'. But it was not to be. By 1968, most of the visitors were between the ages of eighteen and twenty-five. People were coming all the time. The whole summer was given over to a succession of meetings with the general topic of 'Believing'. The meetings were marked by the events which exploded in that fateful year: the shootings on the Square of Three Cultures in Mexico City; the student demonstrations and the month of general strike in France in May; during the summer months, young Czechs in Taizé were to learn one afternoon of the entry of the Russian tanks into Prague; in the United States, Martin Luther King and Robert Kennedy were assassinated, and universities and ghettoes were filled with outbursts of violence.

1969 was the year of shadows. In Biafra a people was being slaughtered. Czechoslovakia was a gaping wound in Europe's conscience. In the Middle East war was raging. For many young people it was impossible simply to stand helpless in the sight of so much injustice across the world. They longed to be part of the decisions affecting their lives. They longed for communication, for their gifts to be put to good use.

On Easter Day 1970, when Brother Roger took the microphone after the young people had spoken, he made the following announcement: 'In order to live out the message we have just heard, one means has imposed itself on us: we are going to hold a council of youth.' In French, the word 'council' is used only for those rare events when the Church

65

throughout the world gathers 'in council'. On that day, no one, including Brother Roger himself, would have been capable of defining what the council of youth was or would become! Yet the intention was clear: let us remain together over a period of time, and try to find ways of making the Easter mystery a reality in our time and place. Announced in 1970, opened in August 1974, the Council of Youth planted the seeds of the 'pilgrimage of trust on earth' that the Taizé Community is currently undertaking with many others around the world. The expression itself was set aside in 1979, perhaps to be taken up again when the occasion for it would arise.

It is most significant that this new stage began on Easter Sunday. 'What has always struck me in Taizé,' a priest from Bolivia told me, 'is the place given to faith in the resurrection of Christ, the trust that the Risen Lord is a source of healing, the answer to the real questions we ask, that he opens new ways forward.'

Perhaps the Resurrection is emphasized so strongly because it reminds us that hope is still possible even in the midst of great suffering, that together we can create a different future. After spending Holy Week in Taizé, a French girl wrote:

'"Christ is risen, Alleluia! He is risen indeed, Alleluia!" How many times did we sing those words in Taizé? I never understood so deeply the meaning of them. Christ is risen, he is alive in each one of us.

'Taizé is a place of meeting, of reflection, between people of different countries, with different stories, different religious backgrounds, united by the same desire for brotherly love. While so many families are torn apart, so many countries and religions divided, people are praying and working for the reconciliation of peoples, for a unity that transcends our differences.

'I left for Taizé hoping to find there a thirst for prayer, for

66

faith. And I discovered the deep significance of reconciliation, that living force of hope called forgiveness. For me now these are not just words. They are the means God gives us to live together in peace and understanding.'

The importance of the paschal mystery is not only felt on the hill of Taizé; it is carried to other places. In the months before a large meeting in a European city or on another continent, for example, a large part of the preparation consists in discovering the signs of hope that already exist in order to share them with those who will arrive. This is a way of helping people to become aware that, in the Church and in the world, signs of resurrection are there for those who know how to recognise them.

In North America, for example, brothers living there began in 1983 a pilgrimage which was to take them to over sixty cities for 'paschal weekends'. They were usually invited by a group of churches, and thus the invitation itself was already a sign of hope, of willingness to seek reconciliation, in a land where the variety of churches often bewilders the visitor from abroad. The weekend often involved visits to 'places of suffering and hope'. The places were discovered and chosen by the local people, and it was always a powerful experience for those concerned. In one small town in Iowa, for example, the person responsible for this was unsure he could find any such places. After searching for a while he came up with over fifty, many more than were needed! In one town, a place of hope was that of an elderly woman who spent time painting portraits of all the 'unsung heroes' of that town and had created an art gallery in her own home for that purpose. One particularly memorable visit was to the Micmac Indian reservation in the town of Restigouche in eastern Quebec. The prayer in the church there was packed, and many whites came over from nearby New Brunswick. After the prayer, the native people invited everyone for a small celebration, during which the children danced traditional dances. The brothers were told that such an evening with native people and whites together was an extremely rare occurrence, 'a kind of miracle', one person said.

At Taizé, every week concludes with the celebration of the paschal mystery, lived out by each person inwardly, but also in the common prayer of the last three days. On Friday evenings, following in the footsteps of some Christians in Eastern Europe, there is a prayer around the icon of the Cross, a chance to bring one's burdens and lay them before Christ, a sign of solidarity with people suffering around the world, particularly prisoners of conscience. Those who wish can place their forehead on the wood of the Cross as a sign that they entrust to Christ all that hurts themselves and others. This prayer was taken up in the meetings outside of Taizé, and soon spread to parishes and communities in different parts of the world.

Saturday evening, the Resurrection is anticipated by a celebration of the light of Christ and by a prayer vigil which may last throughout the entire night. Each person holds a taper in their hand and these are lit one after another while the Gospel is being read, accompanied by a chant of the Resurrection. It is a festival of welcoming into one's own life the light of Christ and of celebrating with the whole Church its vocation to be 'the light of the world'.

The celebration of the Eucharist on Sunday morning, the day of the Resurrection, concludes a week of meetings in Taizé. In this way the Risen Christ, recognised in the Scriptures and in the Bread broken and shared, sends out his disciples to the ends of the earth.

For the past few years, icons of the Cross and of the Resurrection like those in Taizé have travelled on all continents. In a region, a town or a district, the icon of the Cross which had come from Taizé would circulate from a community to a family, from a family to a prayer group, from a prayer group to a prison and then be brought to another region. This practice started spontaneously, as a way of creating concrete and visible links between those who want to live out the paschal mystery in their daily lives. Christ becomes a pilgrim to bring many different people together in all their diversity. 'He will give us enough imagination and courage to open up ways of reconciliation.'

Sometimes this pilgrimage of the Cross leads to surprising discoveries. In Hungary, all of a sudden the icon was not following the planned itinerary; it was lost for several months. People thought it was gone for good when it suddenly reappeared; it had been passed spontaneously from village to village. In Manila (Philippines), it remained for a long time in a prison where several people had been condemned to death. And this news came from Haiti:

'For a prayer around the Cross in Port-au-Prince, we were between two hundred and fifty and three hundred young people and adults. It was a stirring experience for us. Some of the people present, bearing unimaginable suffering, came simply to throw themselves into God's arms. Many people liked the canons, and we even sang some of them in Creole. The pilgrimage of the Cross continued for fifteen days in Port-au-Prince, then went to Cap Haitien. Then it will go to the Dominican Republic. At the end of each week, three separate parishes welcome the Cross for a Eucharistic celebration or a prayer.'

From Northern Ireland: 'To prepare ourselves for the meeting in Paris, we had prayer in the two cathedrals, Protestant and Catholic, one after the other. The Catholic and Anglican bishops came to the two cathedrals to pray with us, and the cross was carried by youth from one church to another. In the midst of such a difficult situation here in our country, the words of St Paul were brought to mind in a concrete, living way: "Christ is our peace; he has made the two peoples one. . . . In his body, he put hostility to death" (Eph. 2).'

From Hong Kong: 'The icon of the Cross began its pilgrimage through China in a parish in Hong Kong. Beginning on Monday, the Cross was passed from family to family. Every day it provided an occasion for a prayer in the homes. Sometimes, before beginning the prayer, people go to visit other families in the same building and invite them. The next day, a member of the family brings the Cross to another house, and on Friday it comes back to the parish. After a while, it goes to another parish.

'One day, we invited all those who had taken part in the pilgrimage to a common prayer. With young people from different denominations, we spent time reflecting on one of the letters from Taizé and then met for a prayer around the Cross followed by the Gospel of the Resurrection. Some twenty young people spent the entire night in prayer in the church. They divided the night into five vigils, one for each continent. At the beginning of the evening, a box had been placed at the foot of the Cross so that everyone could place in it written intentions for prayer. The next day these intentions were distributed among sick people, elderly men and women, and contemplative communities in Hong Kong and Macao. In this way people who could not come to the prayer were able to be part of it.

'Someone left for mainland China to visit his family, and brought the icon of the Cross to his village. He explained the meaning of the pilgrimage. So now, from family to family, a Cross is on pilgrimage in China.'

As part of their pilgrimage across North America, the brothers brought the icon of the Cross to a number of prisons for prayer with the inmates. In California, they visited the maximum security prison in San Quentin, as well as the state medical facility in Vacaville. In 1989, during a visit to the Rio Grande Valley in Texas, they accompanied the Cross to a detention centre close to the Mexican border where undocumented refugees from abroad are held before being sent back to their countries. The churches in this area are doing fine work to offer a welcome to those who cross the Rio Grande river in search of survival and a future for themselves and their families.

In the detention centre, the brothers were able to improvise a short prayer around the Cross outdoors, first with the women and then with the men. Few words were necessary, since the people understood immediately the meaning of the prayer and its relevance to their own situation. They stayed a long time around the icon, kneeling on the grass or on the concrete floor.

With parishes and congregations

The pilgrimage of the Cross made it clear that Taizé was not interested in starting a movement centred upon itself, but wanted to search together with the whole People of God across the earth. 'Make the unity of Christ's Body your passionate concern.' These words from the Rule have always been at the very heart of Taizé's life. We have seen that, in the 1960s, the welcome of young adults not always deeply interested in the Church, to say the least, began to demand more and more of the community's energies. One might have thought that, as a result, the brothers' passion for communion in the Church would be temporarily eclipsed. In fact, exactly the opposite took place. The young people who came to Taizé were not only interested in finding answers for their own lives and in looking critically at what they considered 'inauthentic'; they were also filled with a deep, often unconscious thirst for communication. In Christian terms, this means communion. The challenge for the brothers was to find ways for this desire for communion not to lead merely to the creation of small groups of like-minded people, but to flow into the vast communion of the whole Church and to be a vital force for renewal there.

Already in 1970, the Easter message had taken up the topic of the Church, at a time when protest and revolt seemed to be words heard more than solidarity and trust. And the expression 'council of youth' indicated clearly that the common searching was seen as an event of the Church. In the course of the following years, many young people were sent out across Europe and to other continents to link up individuals and groups, but also to discover, especially in the poorest parts of the world, seeds of a quite different future, seeds of a springtime of the Church.

These visits often led to a discovery of what it means to 'be the Church'. The following letter came from Veronique, a French law student who spent time travelling in Canada: 'I have been in Quebec for over a week now. Each day has been a new occasion for visits and meetings, and a source of astonishment. I feel that I am being carried forward by others, and in fact I think this is indeed the case because of all the many people praying for me. And those I meet are helping me see, each in their own way, the reason I have come here. I have to admit that before leaving I wasn't quite sure! The visits take place with great simplicity, full of the joy of meeting unknown friends, of praying and celebrating together. I am learning in a very concrete way that the members of Christ's Body are many and quite diverse, and that this diversity should be a source of rejoicing. . . . I think I am finally learning to love the Church.'

Discovering and loving the Church is not always easy for young people. It becomes a real challenge when, after a week spent in Taizé, they begin to reflect on how to continue when they return home. As the week comes to an end, regional meetings are organised. At the end of the morning Bible introduction for that day, a brother explains where the different nationalities will meet: the Spanish under the large tent, the Africans in front of the church, the Polish at the Yellow House. . . . In these meetings, the accent is not placed on starting something new but on creating links with already existing realities, of contributing to a renewal of the Church by being leaven in the dough. This involves an emphasis on local parishes and congregations, since these are the places where people do not choose one another, places of continuity where all the generations are present.

Taizé began to speak of the importance of the local parish in the 1970s. At that time, not a few eyebrows were raised in surprise that a monastically-oriented community would take this direction. Later, when the yearly European meetings of young people began, parishes played a great role in the preparation. They offer accommodations to the participants, but more importantly, they are asked to discover signs of hope to share with the many visitors who come from across Europe. During one or two mornings during the European meeting, the participants visit these different 'places of hope': a social-service centre staffed by mothers of the parish, who take care of the daily needs of the poor in the district; a group working against torture in the world; a small fraternity of religious sisters working with young prostitutes, and so on.

The attention to parishes and larger congregations does not mean forgetting the small provisional communities that often spring up overnight. As in other areas, the challenge of Taizé is to try and hold together two realities that seem to be mutually exclusive but should in fact be complementary. The example of the Southern continents has helped the brothers in this regard. Pierre is from Haiti. He has been studying theology in Rome and has spent most of his holidays during the past few years in Taizé. He spoke to me about the small 'ecclesial base communities' so important for the Church in his country. 'These communities take charge of the life of a neighbourhood,' he said. 'They are made up of three to ten persons, and meet once a week in the homes of each of the participants. They reflect on the Word of God, to see how it challenges us in our daily life, they pray together and share the joys and sorrows of the district. In this way people learn that faith in God is not something apart from life, but helps us resist discouragement, share in the sufferings of others and live in solidarity with the most deprived.'

In 1985, the Letter from Madras included a 'Letter to a small community' which spoke of the relationship between these small communities, including even families, and the larger parish:

'If it is rooted in the wider local church community, a small community can be capable of taking risks and of resisting the inertia of discouragement. Even a very few people, three at the least, ten at the most, suffice for such a community to be a living sign of Christ, who gathers us together in order for us to go towards all of humanity.

'The Church is a unique communion which begins where each of us lives. Every home, even if only a single room, can be a "household church". But if that led one to turn in upon oneself, either alone or as a group, it would be causing yet another division. Making your home a household church always involves being ready to go to join the local community of believers where they meet. Otherwise the breath of universality, which means that the Church is a leaven and the soul of society, will be lost.

'If small provisional communities went, at least once a week, to join the prayer of the local church community, it would help us, by a celebration that gathers people of all ages including children and old people, to sense the universality of our communion together. A simple prayer of praise can have great beauty, above all through the singing.

'If local church communities, often called parishes, could

suggest or entrust tasks and responsibilities to the various small communities in their neighbourhood, then a diversity of action would be expressed: some would be asked to visit other communities, others to be particularly attentive to the very poor and isolated, or children who suffer because of broken families, or cultural minorities, or unemployed people who are anxious for their future. Diversity can be constructive if it stimulates us to seek the unanimity of faith.'

The following letter, from three young women living in West Berlin, is a kind of concrete response to this appeal:

'Three of us are living together in a working-class district. Some of the streets look very middle-class, others are almost entirely populated by Turkish people. One of us works with the children, and in this way we have learnt a lot about the living conditions of the families in this town. So many children come from broken homes! Another one of us worked for a while on an assembly-line in a factory with both German and foreign workers. Her work made us realise to what extent resentments, aggressivity and indifference exist at every level in the world of work and production.

'From the start we looked for ways of being in touch with the local parish, and it was not at all difficult. Only elderly people belong to the parishes here. We are young, and so the simple fact of our participating in the worship and other church meetings attracted attention. At the end of our first conversation with the parish priest, he told us, "Just come and live with us. Everything else will grow up naturally". And that is exactly what we wanted to do – simply share the life of the people.'

It should be clear by now that the brothers have always preferred to put action before speaking, to live out themselves what they propose to others. So in 1978, Brother Roger and a group of about twenty brothers went to the town of Bari, in the South of Italy, to live for a time in a tiny parish in 'Bari Vecchia', the oldest part of the city. The parish was made up of a few old women, two or three middle-aged women and a man who helped the brothers set up housekeeping in a few run-down rooms that had been uninhabited for twenty years. During the way, they helped the street-sweepers with their work. It turned out to be a wonderful way to get to know the people in the neighbourhood. Three times each day, as in Taizé, the brothers met for common prayer in the parish church, and at another moment they joined the old women for the recitation of the rosary. Little by little the church filled up, and sometimes in the evening it was packed to overflowing. After the evening prayer, the brothers invited those present for a simple meal, which was often, on account of the numbers, limited to some pasta, a piece of bread and a slice of apple!

When the brothers left the parish, a group of young people from the neighbourhood decided to continue the prayer each evening. Among them were young fishermen, manual labours and many who could find no work. Today, over ten years later, that prayer is still going on! It includes both the recital of the rosary and meditative singing led by the young people. It has led the young people to organise themselves as an 'ecclesial base community' and to take many initiatives, including gestures of sharing with the poor and visits to other communities. That seed planted years ago has found fertile ground.

In 1989, the brothers in the United States had a similar experience, spending ten weeks sharing the life of an African-American parish in the inner city of Milwaukee, Wisconsin:

'St Gall is a poor parish, with one priest and a few parishioners, mostly women, who run everything. For the past twelve years, four times a week, an evening meal has been served to 200 persons, people who are not able to

The pandal: since there was no church big enough for the prayer, a vast bamboo 'cathedral' was improvised for the Madras Meeting (*photo: Taizé*)

A group in one of the parishes, during the Intercontinental Meeting in Madras, December 1985 (*photo: Taizé*)

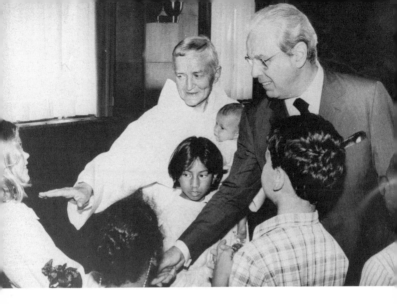

With children from the five continents, Brother Roger presents six questions from young people to Mr Perez de Cuellar, Secretary General of the United Nations (*photo: CIRIC*)

Several of Brother Roger's yearly letters have been written in poor parts of the world. BELOW LEFT: In Calcutta (*photo: KNA*). ABOVE: In Africa (*Lachmann*). BELOW: Haiti (*Taizé*).

European Meeting in Rome, December 1982. Prayer in St Peter's Basilica (*photo: Osservatore Romano*)

European Meeting in London, December 1986
In St Paul's Cathedral (*photo: Taizé*)

The Archbishop of Canterbury and Brother Roger
(*photo: Taizé*)

Meeting in East Berlin, October 1986 (*photo: Taizé*)

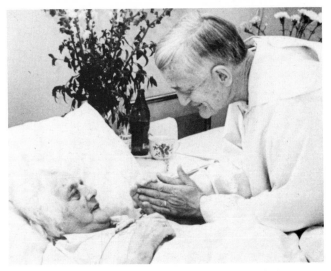

In a hospital in East Germany (*photo: Taizé*)

In a black neighbourhood of a city in South Africa: 'I would like to ask your forgiveness, not in the name of the whites, I could not do that, but because you are suffering . . . so that each of you can make the sign of the cross in my hand, the sign of forgiveness' (*photo: Taizé*)

Taizé, John Paul II at prayer with the young people (*photo: Osservatore Romano*)

Taizé, Pope John Paul meeting with the Community (*photo: Osservatore Romano*)

make ends meet. Most are not church members, but without realizing it, they gradually become a part of the life of the parish. St Gall has also organized a "learning centre", where adults come to learn to read and write. Volunteer teachers from other parishes work with them. Little by little walls fall down; reciprocal trust becomes possible.

'For ten weeks, we gathered in the church for prayer, three times each day. We wondered how our meditative style of prayer would be accepted by people with very different traditions and customs. But because of the growing trust, a way forward together became visible. One day, a woman who came to the prayer every evening said, "This peaceful prayer, and the silence, help me to understand that God looks at me with love, and only love. When I'm tired or angry, I can see God's face in those I take care of, because of the way God looks at me."

'At Pentecost, we celebrated all we had discovered together. The parish invited people from other churches and neighbourhoods. On Friday evening, a prayer around the Cross was held. On Saturday morning, we met in the local Lutheran church for prayer and a Bible sharing on the Beatitudes. In the afternoon, at St Gall, the choirs of the inner-city parishes helped us enter into the prayer of praise so important to African Americans; two parishioners, a young man and the mother of a family, spoke to us of the Beatitudes. The weekend concluded with a festive meal in the place where, every evening, we had served the poor, and a beautiful prayer of Resurrection and of the Holy Spirit. Without realizing it and without many resources, this parish is already living out the deepest reality of the Church, a place of communion for all.'

A Pilgrimage of Trust on Earth

LEBANON. December 1982. Brother Roger is in Beirut to spend Christmas in this country ravaged by war. There have been contacts between Taizé and Lebanon for many years now. Brother Roger has been invited several times, and just recently young Lebanese made a pilgrimage of hope to Taizé.

A question has been preoccupying the founder of Taizé. Three years earlier, the Council of Youth was provisionally interrupted. The numbers of young adults coming to Taizé has been growing, and there was the fear that the Council of Youth would become a 'movement' attached to the community. Better, in that case, to set the expression aside for a time, perhaps taking it up again later for another limited period. But now, at present, what can be proposed to encourage countless young people throughout the world to be bearers of peace, of reconciliation, of trust and of sharing in the situations of our time?

A few days later, meeting with the Lebanese press, Brother Roger announces the opening of a worldwide pilgrimage of reconciliation that will later be called a 'pilgrimage of trust on earth', to last several years and involve young people from every continent. Already in 1980, in a letter he wrote while living among the victims of the earthquake that devastated the South of Italy in that year, Brother Roger urged people to set out as 'pilgrims of reconciliation'. For years, too, young people had been sent out to make visits to individuals, groups, parishes and congregations, to break down walls between people and to celebrate together the mystery of the dying and rising Christ. The brothers themselves had been journeying as pilgrims for a long time, and the meetings organised outside of Taizé had been referred to as pilgrimages. Now all of these smaller pilgrimages would be like rivulets of prayer and communion flowing into a larger river – a pilgrimage of trust across the earth, with stopping-points in many different countries.

When it was announced in Lebanon in 1982, the pilgrimage of trust was thus in fact already underway. Once again, life preceded words. It would now stimulate even more initiatives to overcome oppositions between persons and groups, between races and religions, to create signs of sharing and reconciliation. It would be based on the commitment of the young, but elderly persons, adults and even children would in no way be excluded. Some people would be led to travel far from home, but many others would participate in the pilgrimage in a more hidden way, creating with others signs of hope and peace in their own local situation. Larger gatherings would be stopping-points along the way: prayer celebrations in the capitals of Europe, a European meeting at the end of each year, an East-West meeting held in Hungary, two intercontinental meetings in Madras bringing together young Indians from all parts of the country as well as forty-five other countries, weekly intercontinental meetings in Taizé throughout the summer months. This pilgrimage of trust would also lead Brother Roger to meet with the Secretary General of the United Nations, Javier Perez de Cuellar, in 1985, and to bring to him six questions expressing the aspirations of the young concerning peace and disarmament in the world.

A journey, inward and outward

The 'pilgrimage of trust on earth' took place simultaneously on different levels. The first and most important of these was the most personal. In the *Itinerary for a Pilgrim*, written during a stay among the poor in Chile in 1978, Brother Roger had spoken of the importance of 'an inner pilgrimage lasting an entire lifetime', continually returning to the sources of faith to find the energies to live a life of forgiveness and reconciliation, 'visiting with Christ each of our own prisons [to] see some of the walls fall down [and] spaces of freedom open up'. Without this personal rootedness in the reality of Christ, there could be no hope of a lasting commitment on behalf of others. Taizé had been saying this for forty years.

For many, a week of prayer, sharing and reflection in Taizé is a way of discovering or nourishing this inner pilgrimage. In the same way, the open letters that Brother Roger writes each year attempt to give some key reference-points for a personal journey. The *Itinerary for a Pilgrim*, for example, gives three such lines of force: celebrate the moment with God, struggle with a reconciled heart, accompany Christ by a simple life. In writing these letters, Brother Roger wishes to engage in a dialogue with young people struggling with inner resistances or prey to doubts about God and themselves, yet longing to find the reason and the strength to give their lives to the end.

Starting from this inner pilgrimage, people can find ways to be creators of peace and reconciliation in places both near and far. In the meetings held in Taizé and elsewhere, participants reflect on questions that help them to discover this further dimension: how can I create signs of reconciliations around me? How can I be a peacemaker, even in the midst of tensions, in my local community, in the world? How can we meet one another, visiting and welcoming each other beyond differences and prejudices: Christians and non-Christians, young and old, people of different races and cultures? Can we undertake tiny pilgrimages from one person to another, from one group to another, from one church to another? How can we express our solidarity with the most unfortunate? The questions are not easy, but maybe that is what being a pilgrim means – setting out with few resources, with empty hands.

The following letters provide some 'echoes' of the way young people from around the world have been attempting to respond to Taizé's call to set out on pilgrimage. The situations are the most varied imaginable; the discoveries are the same.

From South Korea: 'Mokpo is a medium-sized city in the South of the country. Its livelihood comes from the sea; there are no large industries. For a long time now the people who live there, for some unknown reason, have been held in contempt by those from other regions of Korea. . . . We left Seoul for Mokpo in the heat of a midsummer day and in the rain of a typhoon, for some "days of reconciliation". Like pilgrims, we left home without knowing what kind of welcome we would find. The welcome in Mokpo was very warm. We organised a prayer every evening, either in a Protestant or in a Catholic church. For the first time, Catholics were welcomed by Protestants and *vice versa*.

'You cannot talk about reconciliation in Korea without bringing to mind the colonial past. At the beginning of the twentieth century, Korea was annexed by Japan and, for a while, even the Korean language was forbidden. Christians took part in the liberation struggle and, in Mokpo, some Church leaders died in that struggle. This reality was present in our celebration, since some Japanese had come to be with us. We prayed, sang and spoke together. And the clouds of our past history were dissipated. "Reconciliation through personal contact, that's what we want," someone said. And the generosity of the Korean heart made it possible.

'The celebration had nothing spectacular about it, but in the joy and silence of prayer, we had the feeling that we had taken a step forward together and passed a turning-point.'

After a visit to some parishes, two young Germans had this to say: 'This kind of visit is important. When we spoke to those whom we met, we realised that they had been waiting a long time for such visits. They were hoping it would provide a new impetus. Many people are at a loss and without ideas when it comes to finding ways to make a parish come alive. Set forms, outmoded traditions, and conflicts between the generations can block from the outset all the roads leading to new vitality. Unless there is a deeply motivated person who is not afraid to take risks, capable of supporting others and of leaping over walls with courage and tenacity. In many cases those living in a situation cannot see the starting-points which already exist. Often all it takes is a word of encouragement or explanation to help them to go further, and to integrate their own contribution into the life of the local Christian community.'

From Bangladesh: 'Our pilgrimage was not one where we had organised a lot of things. The people did not expect that. They were already happy with the fact that you took the trouble to visit them. After the prayer, we had to visit the houses of each participant. Lots of children came with us. The people understood immediately that we had come as simple pilgrims and not to organise big meetings or development projects.'

From Portugal: 'Every week, a small group of us go to a shanty town on the outskirts of Lisbon. Most of the people there come from Cape Verde (islands off West Africa that used to belong to Portugal). We go just to be with them, to listen and to pray together. In Portugal, many Cape Verdeans are rejected by the rest of the population. Their families are very large. Many are building workers and they are usually paid less than the Portuguese. In the neighbourhood we go to visit there are no sewers, and electricity and water supplies are intermittent.

'Around Christmas, we read the Scripture text of the

angels who appeared to the shepherds to tell them of Jesus' birth. Straightaway the eyes of the Cape Verdeans shone with joy, for they identified themselves with the shepherds – they were humble and practically outcast from society, and yet it was to them that the good news was given first of all.'

From Uganda: 'At Mbarara, a city located in the western part of the country, we had a "pilgrimage from hill to hill". Here the people have always constructed their own hills, the Protestants, the Catholics, the Muslims, each with their own hill to defend themselves. Facing one another, the hills each have their own cathedral, schools, hospitals, and surrounding population. At certain times in history there have been contacts and some collaboration, but that has been the exception rather than the rule. It is not religion itself which creates the opposition; denominational differences have been juxtaposed to older tribal and political differences.

'The pilgrimage was prepared by several prayers around the Cross. When the day came we gathered in the middle of the city with several hundred children, young people, students, adults and old people. We sang and then went on our way in silence to Ruharo, the Protestant hill, two hours away.

'At the top of the first hill, which we named the "hill of the beatitudes" for the occasion, we sang and then reflected on the beatitudes. Further on, discovering the mosque, we listened to the promise made to Abraham, our common father in faith. Upon arriving at the cathedral on the Anglican hill, the Anglican bishop welcomed us all, a singing crowd surrounding him. A tropical rainstorm made it necessary to continue singing for over an hour's time.

'The Catholic hill is only a half hour away, as the crow flies, but the two hills are separated by a river and to cross it one must walk two hours. For the occasion, everyone went down straight to the river, crossing it by foot, without using the bridge, in spite of the rain and mud. Climbing the

Catholic hill all the way to the cathedral, some went running to express their desire for reconciliation. The prayer continued there; it was already night-time.

'Relinking these hills with our pilgrimage and crossing the natural boundary formed by the river became signs of reconciliation in which no one had anything to lose or win from others.'

From a journey to Mexico: 'Outside some children are washing themselves in a basin. Next to them, a dog is sniffing at a pile of garbage. Three little girls wander from house to house. Their parents have left: the mother has gone away, the father is an alcoholic. In front of their shack lies a dead scorpion. Nauseating odours make you want to run away. A grandmother tries to lift a baby while a young girl watches her newborn brother. A world of trials, crushed and humiliated.

'In the midst of this desert a rose is blooming. Vicki came here seven years ago. She knows everybody and is in charge of teaching religion to the children. She is a dietician, and gives advice to the mothers. And she is not alone. We visited her with a group of young people who had undertaken the commitment to go to this slum every Sunday.

'After the Council of Youth meetings in Latin America over ten years ago, a period of intense questioning began for the young people here. How can we move beyond indifference? How can we find a commitment to change certain situations? Many have already taken lifelong commitments and still look back to those meetings as to a source.'

From Italy: 'We are writing from a little Italian village. The week we spent in Taizé three years ago opened a whole new path for the young people of the parishes in our area. We started to lead prayer celebrations in the surrounding villages. This has also led to activities of a pastoral and co-operative nature. We would like to be even more attentive to situations where there is a need for leadership and trust.

Concretely, we are helping out in a little parish community next to our own which has no priest. While keeping up our weekly inter-parish time of prayer, we go to lead prayer and meetings for people of all ages in that parish on Saturdays.'

And to close this section, here is Bishop Desmond Tutu, the Nobel Prize winner from South Africa: 'As I worshipped in the Church of Reconciliation in Taizé last year with 5,000 young people from different quarters of our globe, what I can only believe to have been a divinely inspired vision was vouchsafed to me – would it not be wonderful if a pilgrimage of young South Africans of all races could come to Taizé to worship, to laugh, to love, to rough it together as an earnest of our faith in a nonracial South Africa? I was even given the number – 144 from the 144,000 of the blessed in Revelation 7.

'Well, the pilgrimage has happened. Some young South Africans of all races have been to the Holy Land and to Switzerland and then to Taizé. They encountered wonderful hospitality and acceptance. They have returned after sending a message to the Churches in South Africa and after pledging themselves to work for a realisation of our dream.'

From continent to continent

Brother Roger himself has participated in this 'worldwide pilgrimage of trust' in different ways. We have already mentioned his travels to poorer parts of the world. In 1976, two years after the opening of the Council of Youth, the founder of Taizé journeyed to Calcutta and Bangladesh, to spend time living in poor districts along with a group of young people from different continents. A year later, a similar group shared the living conditions of a poor population living in junks on the South China Sea, staying in the harbour of Hong Kong on an old house-boat and in a shack made of scrap wood. These visits resulted in two letters calling upon all Christians to live lives of sharing. Brother Roger continued these journeys in the following years: Mathare Valley (Kenya), Temuco (Chile), a region of southern Italy hit by a severe earthquake, Lebanon, Haiti, sub-Saharan Africa, Ethiopia . . . And before the intercontinental meetings in Madras, he spent time in a poor district of that Indian City.

Brother Roger's choice of a place to stay surprised some young Indians who had come specially to Madras to meet the founder of Taizé. They searched in vain for him in all the hotels of the city, and had given up hope when they happened to glimpse an article from an Indian daily newspaper, *The Hindu*: 'Kutty Street, in the Nungambakkam neighbourhood, is like many other parts of Madras: slums, open drains and mosquitos. And you would certainly not expect somebody well-known to choose this street to live in, even if only for a few weeks. Nevertheless, it is there, in No. 43, that Brother Roger is. And he seems happy to be there. "We are not here for a mission," he said, "but to share the life of the poor."'

It would be fair to say that these visits are a kind of parable. They emphasize that those who are poor and neglected in human terms are not forgotten by God, and that often they are the ones who can show the rest of us a way forward, by the values of trust and sharing they practise so spontaneously. A different kind of parable was given by a visit Brother Roger made in July 1985 to Javier Perez de Cuellar, the Secretary General of the United Nations, in the company of little children from every continent. Brother Roger took this step in the name of all those who are unable to express their opinion regarding the threats to their future. He gave the Secretary General a list of six questions that expressed the hopes of the young for the United Nations to become a creator of trust between the peoples of the earth.

In December 1986, Mr Perez de Cuellar sent the following telegram to Brother Roger: 'As International Peace Year draws to a close and you are once again with a vast ecumenical gathering of thousands of young people in London, I would like them to know that at the United Nations we feel supported by their involvement and their prayer for peace and reconciliation.'

Taizé's concern for the 'Third World' did not mean that another part of the globe escaped their attention, the so-called 'Second World', the countries of Eastern Europe. The first visits by a brother to that part of the world go back some thirty years; in 1962, Brother Christophe travelled in East Germany. Since that time these visits, though until just recently very discreet, have never stopped, and today the community is reaping the harvest of so many years of sowing, as a result of the huge changes now taking place in that part of the world – in the summer of 1990, almost half of all the young people on the hill for the intercontinental meetings came from Eastern Europe and the Soviet Union!

In the early 1980s, meetings of young adults similar to those held in the West took place in East Germany: Dresden, Leipzig, Erfurt, Schwerin, Magdeburg . . . In October 1986, it was Berlin's turn: thousands of young people filled the Catholic cathedral and the Lutheran church called the Marienkirche, in the centre of East Berlin. Cardinal Meisner and the Lutheran bishop Forck joined Brother Roger and the young people in going from one church to the other. The following day Brother Roger went on to Poland, where 6,000 young people were gathered in a church in Warsaw. He was able to make more discreet visits to Hungary and Czechoslovakia as well.

In May 1987, there was a new step forward: a meeting in an Eastern European country that brought together not only young people from those countries, but also young people from the West. This first East-West gathering was held in Ljubljana, the capital of Slovenia, one of the republics of Yugoslavia. Sixty parishes took part in the preparation and, after a few weeks, they had already found room for 4,600 guests!

Two years later, a similar gathering took place in the town of Pécs, in the south of Hungary. The 20,000 participants from Eastern and Western Europe were equivalent to ten percent of the population of Pécs, and so they did not go unnoticed! Fifty neighbouring villages helped with the welcome, and the impressive experience of hospitality was an eloquent sign in a country where for many years mistrust had reigned. After four days in Pécs, a final common prayer was held in the basilica of St Stephen in Budapest, in the presence of the Catholic, Reformed and Lutheran bishops.

In 1988, Brother Roger was invited by the Patriarchate of Moscow to be present for the celebrations of 1000 years of Christianity in that country. In his talks with Russian church leaders, he offered to look for ways of printing bibles in Russian. Accordingly, 'Operation Hope' was reactivated, and less than a year later one million copies of the New Testament in Russian were delivered to Moscow, Kiev, Leningrad and Minsk.

At the end of 1989, it was possible to have a European meeting in Eastern Europe, in Wroclaw in Western Poland. Between the announcement of the meeting at Pécs and the time it actually took place, incredible changes took place in one Eastern European land after another. This also changed the complexion of the gathering. 42,000 young adults from outside Wroclaw, from the Atlantic Ocean to the Urals, came together there for five days. Outside the railway station they were greeted by a large banner saying, 'Solidarnosc welcomes Taizé'. They were all welcomed into families, and afterwards there were still places left! Common prayers were held simultaneously in seven large churches, two sport halls and four circus tents, and all the languages of Europe rang out in the dusty streets of that industrial town. During one of the common prayers, Brother Roger said, 'These days, we have seen an intuition confirmed: Europe will be built through the trust coming from faith, which is so vital after these years of mistrust, fear and violence.' This was confirmed by messages of good-will from Polish prime minister Tadeusz Mazowiecki, Czechoslovakian president Vaclav Havel, UN secretary general Perez de Cuellar and Pope John Paul II. The following year, Prague would be the site of a similar European meeting.

In a very different context, but one in which signs of reconciliation and communion are equally important, a similar gathering was held in Ireland in May 1985. On the first day of the meeting, five thousand participants filled three large churches in Dublin: the Roman Catholic cathedral, the ancient cathedral of the Church of Ireland and a third church in a poor neighbourhood. When Brother Roger spoke in one of the churches, he could be heard simultaneously in the other two. An Irish newspaper remarked that it was the first time that churches of different confessions were linked together in this way.

Several hundred young people came from Northern Ireland for the meeting. For some Protestants from the North, it was the first time they had ever entered a Catholic church, and the opposite was true as well. The Catholic archbishop and leaders of the other churches took part in the prayers, and a preparation lasting several months and including a daily prayer in the centre of Dublin helped to involve many parishes and to discover many signs of hope that the participants were able to visit during the meeting. 'I never saw my church so full,' said one of the priests from the Catholic cathedral, 'and yet the mass media hardly spoke about the preparation.'

European meetings

It is now time to turn to an aspect of the 'pilgrimage of trust on earth' already mentioned several times in passing: the European meetings that, at the end of each year, bring together tens of thousands of young adults from across Europe for several days. From 1978 to 1988, before the larger gatherings in Eastern Europe, these meetings were held in London, Paris, Barcelona, Rome and Cologne.

The accent of the European meetings lies on sharing the life of the Church in a given city. Participants spend four or five days living, worshipping and reflecting together with the Christians there, entering into the life of their neighbourhoods and parishes. On the first day, until late at night, thousands of young pilgrims arrive in the city, invading the railway and underground stations, the bus lines and the parishes. For the Rome meeting, a caravan of twenty special trains entered *Stazione Termini* at the same time, and the station was suddenly crowded with people young and old speaking every imaginable language. In London, *The Times* reported that it was the largest one-night crossing of the Channel since the Second World War. In Paris, as the morning passed, the church being used as a welcome centre became so full that the only space left was in the chapel set aside for silent prayer, while the closest *métro* station had run out of tickets!

Welcoming so many people at the same time is not easy. In London, drivers were caught in a traffic jam in front of Westminster Abbey. All the coaches were discharging their passengers there, and a multicoloured crowd was heading in all directions towards the places of welcome set up according to languages. Once the participants reach these places, the different possibilities for the meeting are explained, and people are sent to the places where they will be staying. This has to be done as quickly as possible, since people are tired after a long journey. The 5,000 Spanish who came to

London had to travel for three days, and the Finns who came to Rome had to take two ferries and travel thousands of kilometres. And often those who arrive do not speak a single word of the language of the country, so from the start it is truly a pilgrimage of trust!

'We began work very early in the morning,' a girl who had been part of the welcome team told me. 'It was still dark when we got to the place of welcome, but already several hundred people were there waiting for the doors to open. They had spent the whole night travelling. There were a hundred of us to welcome them. Fifty of us had worked for several hours the evening before to put up signs, get the rooms ready, and prepare the thousands of meal and transportation tickets needed.'

But before any of this can happen, a long preparation is necessary. Shortly after Easter, those who are in charge of preparing the meeting go from one parish and community to another in the city that has been chosen. A conversation with the person in charge, a contact with the groups of the parish, a simple prayer service together. . . . and things are underway. Little by little, a network of contacts grows up in the city. In each parish, families offer to welcome one, two, five or more pilgrims; some give up their winter vacations in order to be present for the meeting; families who will be out of town for Christmas leave their house-keys with friends. . . .

In each parish, groups are formed to take charge of the welcome, to organise the families, to reflect on how to make the meeting a meaningful event for the whole parish, to look for signs of hope to share with those who will come. Often this preparation helps break down walls within the parish – between young and old, between different tendencies, and so on. By the time the meeting itself arrives, the local Church generally discovers that it has much more to share with those who arrive than it had suspected beforehand.

A group from Barcelona wrote: 'For us, preparing to hold

91

a European meeting in our city means making ourselves available simply to welcome those who will come to visit us in a spirit of pilgrimage. Our group has existed in the parish for quite some time. We meet each week to pray. It is an occasion on which we rely so as to be able to make reconciliation in our families, the city and the Church a reality. We wondered how we could live out our pilgrimage in a special way in the months before the meeting.

'We are visiting the families who will be welcoming participants from other countries. Each week we meet in a different house for prayer, as an encouragement in our common search and to discover God's gifts in one another. For these families, opening their door involves an inner transformation, sowing a seed of trust in their own hearts and accomplishing a little sign of hospitality and sharing in today's world.

'Our neighbourhood, in the heart of the city, has its problems. There is an alarming unemployment rate which destroys hope. Many disillusioned young people turn to drugs and find themselves rejected by others who hide behind indifference. The European meeting can be a good opportunity to try to hope together, to have confidence for the future and to live in the present moment, rooted in the Risen Christ.'

Another group wrote: 'Here in Mataro, preparing ourselves for the European meeting has made us discover that even very committed people are unaware of the actual dimensions of certain problems in their neighbourhoods: unemployment, delinquency, drugs and poverty. The preparation for the meeting must mean an openness towards our surroundings: seeing what is really there and not imagining what we would like to see. What can we do to be a welcoming Church and to let even the most sceptical find in the Church the beginnings of friendship? We have to find people who are already committed in these situations, groups and individuals who give the best of themselves.

'While doing all this work, another form of preparation for the meeting is a prayer which we have held each week for four years. It is a chance to feel welcomed and to place before God all that has happened during the week. Time permitting, there is prayer together each morning before work or study. This started on our return from the Cologne meeting last year, and it will continue after the meeting in Barcelona.'

At the same time as all this goes on in the city where the meeting will be held, a similar preparation is undertaken throughout Europe. Often all it takes is a small core-group to get many others interested. Sometimes this group begins meeting in a parish or at university, and decides at the end of the summer to start a pilgrimage of trust in their own situation, with their families, friends and neighbours. In some places, young people go on pilgrimage from parish to parish, inviting the members of each congregation to meet for a time of prayer together. They visit different ethnic groups and invite them to take part. Sometimes, this prayer is followed by a time of sharing. The adults discover what the young people's motivations are and their expectations of the Church; the young learn to leave behind many pre-judices and to realise that communion in the Church is only possible if all the generations participate together.

During the European meeting itself, all the participants come together at midday and evening for common prayer. 'When, in the magnificent cathedral of Cologne, one of the largest in the world,' wrote a participant, 'a crowd of young people spent over ten minutes in utter silence during a prayer celebration, the fundamental reason why they were there became almost tangible. They had come together for five days to search for God together. After the silence, the singing started up again. The simplicity of the Taizé chants works well with a small group. But ringing out under the arches of a vast cathedral, they take on an amplitude that can unify a great crowd despite the differences of language.'

In Paris, three huge churches – Notre Dame, Saint Sulpice and Saint-Germain-des-Prés – were used for the prayers during the five-day-long meeting. In Rome, on the evening of 30 December, the prayer with Pope John Paul II had the same format as the prayer of the preceding days in the other basilicas of Rome. But in St Peter's it took on a quality all its own. For four hours straight, the basilica, filled to overflowing, resounded with canons and meditative songs that began a long time before the Pope's arrival. The icon of the Cross stood at the foot of the altar. 'It is not often the case that St Peter's Basilica is too small to hold all those who come there to pray,' commented a Roman newspaper the next day. As a matter of fact, ten thousand people had to remain outdoors and, after the service, the Pope went to the balcony to greet them. It was the first time that St Peter's was filled with people of so many different denominations, and young people at that.

Here is how one observer described the first European meeting in London, in late 1981: 'In the biggest single crossing of the English Channel since the Second World War, 17,000 young Europeans ferried across one night. Wearing coloured parkas and rugged shoes and carrying rucksacks, they converged on London to meet another 3,000 young people from England, Scotland, Wales and Ireland. Together they took over three of London's principal buildings – St Paul's Cathedral, Westminster Abbey and Westminster Cathedral. Walking into St Paul's Cathedral on the first night of the "occupation", I was stunned to see thousands of young people covering the entire floor of the huge church, sitting in small groups around a cluster of candles in semi-darkness. The sound of their plaintive, repetitive, almost Oriental chanting rose and fell like the wind on a mountainside. In a building associated with the most formal celebrations of the Church of England (like the royal wedding five months earlier), the crowd of youth would have seemed anarchistic, except for the powerful tide of worship.' At the second London meeting, in 1986, the Archbishop of Canterbury along with other Church leaders participated in the prayer around the Cross in St Paul's, as did Cardinal Hume two days later in Westminster Cathedral. Every evening, Brother Roger's meditation was heard in all the churches, this time including St George's Cathedral, and then he went from church to church to join the young people in prayer.

But beyond the large prayer services and the great crowds, it is the multitude of small personal encounters that touch the participants in the European meetings. As a result of being welcomed into families and sharing in the life of parishes, many have an experience unlike any other.

'We were quite a mix of nationalities that came to stay in a parish in a working-class district of Rome,' wrote one participant. 'We were from Spain, France, Holland, Britain, Austria and Germany. Those who welcomed us were not very well-off and lived in small homes. But there was room for us all. And above all, they made room in their hearts. They showed us a friendliness and an openness that was really something extraordinary.'

In the mornings, throughout the city, the participants make the visits that have been prepared for them. There are discoveries that are sometimes painful, but also full of hidden hope. 'During the London meeting,' someone wrote, 'we were invited to discover places of suffering and hope, so I chose to visit a shelter for homeless people. "Christ loves us just as we are, so we welcome those who come just as they are: tramps, alcoholics, prostitutes, and so on; that is our programme," explained a smiling Methodist minister to us. "These women and men had jobs, families, responsibilities, then everything fell apart. Now they are alone, they have a little money but they do not accept themselves as they are. So our job is to love them."'

Such meetings build bridges between races and cultures: 'In the district that welcomed us, there are many Asian people. On New Year's Day, Bengali families came and prepared a traditional meal for us in the parish centre. We shared the meal, but a deeper sharing also took place, a step from mistrust towards trust. One of the families had taken the risk of bringing a child who had been attacked and beaten by whites, and whose attitude at the beginning of the meal was one of fear and suspicion. Seeing him change in the course of the meal was one of the small miracles of this pilgrimage of trust.'

Those who were staying in the small town of Siegburg, near Cologne, visited the prison for youth. It is the largest one in Europe, holding 850 young men. For several years, young people from the town have been in contact with the prisoners, and they prepared a celebration in the prison chapel. Were it not for the fact that some people were wearing grey, you could not have told who the inmates were! The chaplain said later that the prisoners were visibly moved by the event.

In Rome, all the participants went to pray in the catacombs. 'On 31 December,' one group said, 'we met together from several different parishes. Five hundred of us walked across fields till we reached the catacombs. It was a pilgrimage to the sources of our faith and to a Church that is a land of simplicity, humility and reconciliation.' This pilgrimage to the sources is also accomplished each day during the meeting by a moment of reflection together on a Bible text.

The European meetings are organised without subsidies or funding. Everything is accomplished using very simple means. The Archbishop of Canterbury was visibly struck by this: 'Normally during our Church meetings, it takes a lot of money to bring together one thousand participants. You have done much more with very little!' As in Taizé, each participant contributes something and that must suffice. But the simplicity of means is a road to freedom: in London, Barcelona and Rome, were not the poorest families the ones who offered the warmest welcome?

As with all the meetings organised by the Taizé Community, the full import can only be understood afterwards. People's lives have been touched, and that inevitably bears fruit, if often in ways hard to measure. 'I knew hardly anything about Taizé besides the name,' a parish priest in London said after the meeting. 'It's the first time I have ever experienced such a gathering. Something in my parish will change. We are going to continue the prayer. There are many prayer groups here but only for people over 40; the young do not attend.' He also spoke about the meetings between churches involved in the preparation; 'We meet each week with the Anglican priests and the Methodist ministers, but our congregations have had very few contacts. They had to work together to prepare the European meeting, and that is something else that will continue here.'

Since the first meeting in Barcelona in 1979, a weekly prayer has brought together several hundred people in a large church in the centre of town. In Paris, too, since 1983, a daily prayer is held in St Germain-des-Prés. 'This prayer,' said Pascal, one of those who help organise it, 'is in the heart of the Latin Quarter. In a side chapel of the church we have placed an icon of the Cross and some candles. Every day someone else prepares the prayer. Its regularity and the fact that it is open to all enables students, tourists and working people to meet and to create, in the midst of a busy city, a few moments of quiet and of reflection, a space of peace.' A similar prayer began in a Romanesque church in the centre of Cologne after the meeting there. Each day a group from a different parish takes charge of it.

Those who return home after the European meetings also find the courage to take new initiatives. A group from

Germany wrote to Taizé: 'We were deeply affected by the prayers around the Cross during the London meeting. Here we meet every Friday in a church for such a prayer. We have invited some foreigners to join us – they are people who have asked for asylum in Germany and who at present are living in an old army barracks. Many of them speak no German; they feel isolated, and a bit lost and bewildered in the face of a powerful bureaucracy. The prayer around the Cross is a tiny beginning of hope for them. It gives them a possibility to escape their isolation. Through their presence we are learning that solidarity is not just a question of praying; prayer leads us to become involved in concrete actions.'

Often, people in a neighbourhood come together for 'reconciliation meetings'. They attempt to discover the problems caused by divisions in their neighbourhood, family or parish. One group wrote: 'Christ has called us to build up the communion of the Church. But we create barriers in our local communities and so create a caricature of that Church. The European meeting gave us the desire to make our own communities an image of the universal Church. We cannot say that we found ready-made solutions in Barcelona, but we have begun to set out to deal with our problems in a new way.'

Madras: an intercontinental meeting

On 27 December 1985 at 5 a.m., the neighbourhood of Nungambakkam in Madras saw an incredible movement of people. They were heading across the large avenue of Sterling Road, bordered by slums, to the door of the Jesuit University, which welcomed this chaos with great generosity.

Most of these people were young, and they had come from all over India, even the most distant parts (Assam and

98

Meghalaya, north of Bangladesh). About a thousand others came from twenty Asian countries and most of the countries of Europe. There were even a few from other continents. It was a colourful crowd, discovering its diversity with amazement: the intercontinental meeting in Madras was about to begin.

Christians from India, among them Church leaders, had asked the brothers of Taizé to prepare this meeting, insisting that it not be limited to Asians. 'We need a meeting in Asia to which young people come from the entire world,' one of them said upon visiting Taizé.

No other pilgrimage gathering had ever had such a long preparation. Eighteen months earlier some Taizé brothers, also from different continents, were there to make the first contacts. They rode their bicycles from one end of Madras to the other. Then several Sisters of St Andrew, including one of Asian origin, came to live for a year in a small house in Nungambakkam. The two communities were quite small given the size of the task before them. But they were counting on the creativity and the know-how of the youth of India. Each month, a day of prayer and reflection was held for young people from throughout the city. Small groups were formed in different districts to stimulate the welcome in families. People began really to learn to receive and to share.

'This meeting will be an adventure of trust,' said Brother Roger. 'It is still an unknown. In particular, we do not have the material means to organise it.' The preparation involved visits to other places as well. In the summer before the meeting, young people from different countries set out by twos to cross the Indian subcontinent. In this way, before the meeting even began, links could be forged between young Indians and young people from Europe and other continents. One French girl who was involved in these visits wrote:

'I set out with two words in my backpack: listen and invite. Nothing more. When I arrived, I added a third: share. Our means were very limited. In addition, we were in an unknown world, a totally different civilisation; we did not know how to do the simplest things: post a letter, use the telephone, take the train. . . . What a funny feeling for Europeans used to efficiency! We had to learn everything all over again. So that made us not organisers from Europe, but pilgrims.'

At the same time, young people, alone or in groups, were preparing to set out on pilgrimage to Madras, or to find ways of participating in the meeting while staying at home. Those who left for Madras discovered the meaning of the word 'pilgrim' in a very concrete way. Many celebrated Christmas Eve on the road. At Kuwait, some held a small prayer in the airport lounge. In Damascus, others were able to use a separate room in the airport to pray a bit longer. On the train from Delhi to Madras, a Polish priest celebrated Midnight Mass for thirty-eight Polish pilgrims, and many other people spontaneously joined the celebration.

The government granted the young Indians who participated a 50 per cent reduction on their railway tickets. Many came from very poor villages, and had to travel a long way. A special train for a thousand Indians was organised from the state of Bihar, in the North. Most were aided by their group, parish or movement with the costs of the journey, as a concrete way of sharing in the pilgrimage. To welcome the pilgrims, Madras offered the best of what she had: openness of heart and the grace of sharing. Most of the young people were welcomed into families. So as not to be a load on the family hosting them, the participants brought back with them portions of cooked rice which had been distributed at the meeting place, wrapped in a banana leaf.

Every group in Madras prepared for this welcome with generosity and seriousness. One of the groups had started by reflecting at length on the meaning of welcoming a guest, and a foreigner besides. Their neighbourhood, Shastrinagar, is very poor; its population of Tamil origin has been through several exiles, the last time having been driven out of Burma. Bit by bit they discovered that it was important to welcome the foreigners as if they were Indians, letting them learn, even clumsily, to eat with their right hand, to sit and to sleep on mats on the ground, etc. These would be the best conditions for a real meeting. And since many of the houses of the district are very poor, they had the idea of building a shelter together, over which they stretched fabric. The families were anxious to welcome the foreigners for meals.

From the four corners of the earth, pilgrims set out without knowing where they would be staying. And the people of Madras opened their doors without knowing who they would be welcoming. For most of the pilgrims from Europe, North America, Australia and the Pacific, it was their first experience of the Third World. For some of the Indians, the attitude of their guests was quite a shock: 'They sit and sleep on the ground, they don't complain about the food, they don't watch television and they come early to the prayer,' said one girl from Bombay. 'What am I doing here alongside them?'

Each morning the pilgrims converged, from all the suburbs of this city of over three and a half million people, on to the University of Nungambakkam, which is surrounded by a huge area of fields and trees. There they spent the daytime, which was especially marked by the two periods of common prayer, each lasting an hour and a half. As there is not a cathedral large enough to hold so many people in Madras, an enormous 'pandal' was prepared, a temporary structure of bamboo and matted coconut leaves, usually erected in front of a house for a wedding feast or a traditional festival in India. It was splendidly decorated: great

101

quantities of oil lamps and vigil lights, blossoms and pottery surrounded an icon of the Cross, always draped with fresh garlands of flowers, with sticks of incense burning in front. This was the sacred space of the meeting, a place of silence filled with the echoes of an extremely noisy city.

In this temporary cathedral, the two common prayers of the day took place. During the first chant, a little child or a young girl dressed in a sari would go to light the Indian lamp, symbol of the light of God. Taizé chants in English, Indian chants in Tamil, solos in different languages, short readings, ten minutes of silence, and at the end a short meditation by Brother Roger in English, translated into Tamil and Hindi, and then simultaneously into thirty other languages. In India, where multilingualism often leads to real conflicts, this diversity of languages in the same liturgy was a surprise. The neighbours of one family involved in the meeting decided to come to the prayer themselves when they heard it was in all the languages.

The crowd sank into prayer while the noise of the city never ceased. The silence penetrated each person and contributed to the seriousness of the times of small-group sharing with topics like: 'How can we break with fatalism and passivity of all sorts in the face of divisions?' 'What risks can we take to make the earth a place fit to live in, concretely, in our own surroundings?' There was the discovery that words like 'liberation' or 'freedom' did not at all have the same meaning from one continent to another, but that nonetheless, the same search was present in a great diversity of expressions.

Such an experience caused a lot of prejudices to fall, in particular in the relationships between young people from the cities and young people from the countryside, between different Christian denominations, between Indians and Westerners. Singhalese met with Tamils at a time when, in

Sri Lanka, the two groups were at war. High-caste people were able to share with others from lower castes.

Those who arrived ahead of time were able to share even more deeply the reality of India by spending time in the villages around Madras or in Kerala. They saw that the life of most Indians consists in a struggle for survival, and this made the warmth and generosity of the welcome in the villages even more amazing. A young Filipino wrote: 'I was in Madras. I now realise that taking part in that meeting was a big preparation for facing the situation in my country today. Now is the moment for me and for many others to be bearers of trust!

'Before the elections took place, our bishops wrote a pastoral letter strongly urging us to be united in defence of the life of our country, and to stand up for the truth. The response which this evoked quickly became clear. Thousands of volunteers from all walks of life dedicated time and energy to try to ensure that the elections would be honest, at the risk of their social position and even their lives. It was impressive. As well as that involvement, we gathered for prayer vigils and meetings to deepen our commitment.

'The challenge to live out our faith and to recognise it as the driving force of all our action for justice has become clearer than ever. After the elections persecutions against the Church have continued. But for us, with all the people of the Philippines who have such a deep faith, that is something which purifies.'

From Rome: 'In Madras there was the common prayer, the meetings and the small groups. And then there was all that I discovered in others and in my own heart after so much fear and inner panic. All that helped my hope and generosity to emerge: no longer the fear of committing my own life to search for greater sharing in the face of misunderstanding, but the joy of committing myself in this way and of making it known.'

Abraham from Kerala: 'It was marvelous to see on the early morning of the 27th, hundreds and thousands of young people arriving from all over the globe. Just like the Ganges and the Yamuna merge at the Confluence of Agra, the East and the West were merging as one at Madras. Thousands of young people from different corners of the world being hosted in hundreds of houses and communities for about eight days: this was just wonderful. Is there a better parable of sharing? It was magnificent to see European girls wearing Indian sarees and the cultural interaction that took place in Madras. The impact of this meeting on the Indian youth and our church leaders is really amazing. The prayer was the most beautiful part. Now for the first time, a meeting where people are not classified according to their denominations. We know it is possible to work together and do something to dispel the darkness.'

Following the meeting, the Catholic bishops of India wrote in their annual report, 'The significant event of 1985 was the International Meeting held by the Taizé brothers at Madras in collaboration with us. It was the first time in the history of the Church in India that so many young people were gathered together.' This led to a second intercontinental meeting in Madras sponsored by the Catholic bishops together with the United Church of South India, from 27 to 31 December 1988. Ten thousand young adults from twelve states of India, together with young people from all the continents, came together at the same time as 33,000 others were meeting in Paris. Taizé's 'pilgrimage of trust on earth' was continuing to sow seeds of inner life and international solidarity.

Life-long Commitment

LET'S SIT down here for a minute. Here, on this bench in the middle of the village. If we wait a few minutes, we are bound to see people arriving or leaving. There is someone, just coming up the hill now. And here come two others, on their way down to catch the bus to Chalon. With this constant coming and going, do you think it is possible to draw conclusions about Taizé? The people you find here today will be on their way home soon; others will be arriving, with other backgrounds, other ideas. You would have to spend a whole year here – but even then, what could you write? Of course, a few people stay longer at Taizé, to help welcome the others and organise the meetings. But they too come and go.

Only the brothers have nowhere else to go. Only they could say that Taizé is the place of their every-day living. One day, perhaps they will feel called to go to live somewhere else; but they would go there together. Their lives are set in common, because they have been given to Christ. They are monks. By their once-for-all commitment, by the contemplative vocation, the undivided love. They are very modern monks, though, with their travels and their concern for peace and sharing. Nothing must make us forget that they have a first priority in life which is of the order of the Invisible. Out of their celebration of the invisible Reality grows their acute understanding of what they see happening in the world today, and their refusal to turn their backs on the world.

Commitment is gift of oneself. No one can give themselves totally overnight. Each of the brothers has had early years in the community when he learned the consequences of his vocation, and found how to face them. Then, after four or five years of preparation, he was ready to say yes to Christ's call. Yes to Christ, in the community of his brothers and in common with them. Yes to community of goods – be they material things or spiritual gifts. Yes to a life in celibacy. Yes to the ministry of a 'servant of communion' at the centre of the community's life. Yes to a life of which nothing can be known in advance. A gift, a 'yes' that is not taken back. The brothers are the first to live the words of Brother Roger's letter 'A Life We Never Dared Hope For':

'You open up the way of risk. You go ahead of me along the way of holiness. . . . You ask me, not for a few scraps, but for the whole of my existence. . . . One day I understood: you were asking me to commit myself to the point of no return.'

It is not enough to mention the promises made by the brothers. How are they understood and lived? A careful reading of the Rule of Taizé may help us to understand.

The servant of communion

'To avoid encouraging any spirit of rivalry, the servant of communion is responsible before his Lord for making decisions without being bound by a majority. Set free from human pressures, he listens with the same attention to the most timid brother as to a brother full of self-assurance. If he senses a lack of real agreement on an important question, he should reserve judgement and, in order to advance, make a provisional decision, ready to review it later; standing still is disobedience for brothers advancing towards Christ.'

We are reminded of what Saint Benedict said of the abbot's task, its difficulty, and of the need for him to be a father of all, adapting the various gifts and needs of each member to the life of the whole community. This is even clearer in the lines which describe the ministry of the servant of communion in more detail:

'Without unity, there is no hope for bold and total service of Jesus Christ. Individualism breaks up the community and brings it to a halt.

'The servant of communion inspires unity within the community.

'Each brother should frankly tell the servant of communion, in private, the fears he may have. Revolt expressed before others is bound to contaminate.

'The servant of communion is subject to the same failings as his brothers. If they love him for his human qualities, they risk no longer accepting him in his ministry when they discover his faults.

'Making decisions is a formidable task for the servant of communion.

'He should look for the special gifts of each brother, so that the brother can discern them for himself.

'He should not consider his charge to be superior, nor must he assume it in a spirit of resignation. He should bear in mind only that it has been entrusted to him by Christ, to whom he will have to give account.

'He should arm himself with mercy and ask Christ to grant it as the grace most essential for him.'

Do we realise what a new vision of authority this is? For us the word implies 'being in charge' or even 'having power over others'. Here this is not so, and though the 'crisis of authority' in the Church in recent years may have made us more receptive to this vision, think how revolutionary such language was in 1952! What are the implications for the Church of this approach? In one of his early books, Brother Roger was to write:

'In common life, is the majority system really the best? It is always permissible to express doubt when the Church simply borrows a procedure from human society. Is the will

107

of the Lord clear if fifty-one per cent are in favour of something? In the Church, decisions are taken in order to follow the path traced out for us by God and to lead Christians along a way of practical service. Authority in a community can only be Christ-centred.

'This ministry has nothing to do with human constraint, or the imposing of one's own will. It can never take the place of another's conscience; its role is to recall the will of Christ. A servant of communion must be on the watch against that secret form of ambition which consists in a desire to dominate souls and make them our own.

'The ideal would be to make all decisions on a unanimous basis. But idealism is not an evangelical notion. If we always had to wait for everyone to agree before we advanced, the community would very soon be at a standstill. It is vital to keep moving ahead; whoever tries to stop begins to regress.'

In creation's simple beauty

The word 'poverty' is not used in Taizé to speak of the life of the community, out of respect for all those whose lives are wounded by grinding poverty and wretchedness. Like the first Christians in Jerusalem, the Rule calls the brothers to have 'everything in common':

'The pooling of goods is total.

'The audacity involved in putting to good use all that is available at any time, not laying up capital and not fearing possible poverty, is a source of incalculable strength.

'Poverty has no virtue in itself.

'The poor of the Gospel learn to live without having the next day's needs ensured, joyfully confident that everything will be provided.

'The spirit of poverty does not mean looking poverty-stricken, but disposing everything in creation's simple beauty.

'The spirit of poverty means living in the joyfulness of each present day.'

In a world sensitive to 'life-style' and outward symbols of wealth, the community strives to live out this vision seriously: giving up the ownership of its fields, making no investments, refusing any gifts or donations. What strikes the visitor to Taizé is often a certain 'style'. In the Church of Reconciliation, or in the 'Yellow House' where visitors arrive, or in 'El Abiodh', the guest-house run by the Sisters of St Andrew, details make all the difference in the overall atmosphere. 'Poverty' in religious communities is sometimes confused with drabness, a refusal of all that is light and fresh and cheerful. Here the spirit of poverty means simplicity and festival, expressed with the poorest means – a few flowers, a candle. It is never excessive ostentation.

In our modern, affluent societies, belongings are offered as a way of security, a happiness that money can buy. No doubt the brothers could have grown very rich, if they had wanted to. The community is still young and dynamic; its members have gifts rarely found in such concentrated harmony. Brother Roger once expressed that risk: 'If we only worked to produce what we need for ourselves, we would be making a mistake. If we were not determined to give away portions of our income, either we would work less and less or we would become very rich.'

People today are very sensitive about the wealth of the Church, and the Churches are not always at ease in answering the challenges. In Taizé, where little is said of the financial situation, there is a constant struggle to balance the budget. The brothers are not production-minded, and yet the community has to live, and never be dependent on gifts or outside funding. Some costs are vital for its ministry – postage and communications, for example; how to be in contact with people all over the world without letters, telephone calls, and even a telex? Then there are all the journeys to join young people throughout the world. There are the brothers in the fraternities on different continents. And in recent years, there are the costs of welcoming so many visitors to Taizé, costs that are not always completely covered by the contributions of those who come. A sudden wind- or hail-storm may destroy a number of tents, and wreak havoc with that year's accounts.

Taizé offers an attitude to work that is radically different to the one we normally have. The goal of the brothers' work is not to make life comfortable for themselves. The first goal is to ensure freedom in their ministry; independence is vital, and so is the ability to have something to share with others – and not only superfluous left-overs. Among the brothers, there are some whose work brings income, while others work without remuneration – writing letters, talking with guests, studying and writing, organising the youth meetings and pilgrimages – but there is no superiority of one kind of work over the other. Both are aspects of the common ministry of the community.

The community's income derives mainly from the different workshops. From the earliest years of its existence, the brothers developed a pottery-workshop where a number of brothers work either full- or part-time, transforming the clay and plants of the region into simple stone-ware of great artistry. Other brothers make enamel crosses or pendants, or take photographs which are turned into postcards. The community has always had artists and craftsmen among its number. And then there are the books written and printed by brothers at 'les Presses de Taizé'. Books of theology, of spirituality, of poetry, of pottery-lore, often translated and published in many different languages.

At Taizé, the concept of 'work' is never divorced from the attempt to discern the gifts of each brother. The ministry of the community can vary, and so the possibilities may change too. But the first question when a new brother comes to join

110

the community, always someone in his twenties, is not 'What is he trained to do?' but 'Who is he really?' The question of a brother's work becomes the question of the service of Christ which he is being called to accomplish. Here we are invited, in the Church, to rediscover the meaning of the concept of 'the priesthood of all believers', the vocation of every Christian to live Christ for others, according to the gifts received and the vocation responded to.

A life-time in celibacy

'Whoever loses his life for my sake will find it.' Losing and giving our life goes in the direction of the Gospel's radicalism, not along with the current infatuation with 'self-fulfilment'. How else can we understand something of the Gospel vocation to celibacy? No subject is more delicate, and Brother Roger has written in various places how in the early days, that aspect of the brothers' commitment estranged sympathy among Protestant friends more than any other. All the Reformation Churches rejected celibacy categorically, and the explicit commitment of the brothers to a lifetime of celibacy was a real innovation. It is hard to explain this complete silence over a possible form of Christian vocation, which Brother Roger has often put in relationship with the vocation of marriage, the two absolute commitments for love in the Church needing one another to be understood aright.

In the Catholic Church this commitment was familiar, and perhaps it explains the ready agreement to the presence of Catholic brothers in Taizé. In 1971, Brother Roger sent the Pope a message in which he attempted to express the present-day value of celibacy as a positive sign in the Church:

'Celibacy is a life of Gospel folly, and it is seen as such by

111

humanity, but it proclaims the coming Kingdom and stimulates the Church of God to live to the full its vocation to be the salt of the earth.

'Celibacy is certainly not an easy way to follow; in it women and men give their entire lives to Christ, without keeping back anything for the future. And by it they "receive a hundredfold with persecutions", often a matter of inner struggle on behalf of all those people God entrusts to their pastoral keeping. Celibacy does not deny in any way the sanctity of Christian marriage; on the contrary, it stimulates each Christian to discover what a specific vocation the laity is called to, that 'royal priesthood' in every Christian's life which invites us to live Christ for others. That means that in the future, Christians are going to exercise much more explicitly a share in the Church's common ministry.'

And Brother Roger adds: 'Celibacy has always kept a mystical element alive at the very heart of the Church's life – always the Church was being invited to look towards the invisible, the mystery of Christ, the non-rational life of the Gospel.' What can we say of the present-day arguments, so often heard, that man and woman are necessary for one another's fulfilment, that a life of celibacy is an inhuman privation? Such a question would need more time to answer properly, but it is not hard to find experts in human psychology who would warn against any such over-simplifications. As though every married person were happy, and every celibate servant of Christ neurotic and unfulfilled! Experience proves that this is not so. The tensions, frustrations and difficulties of life in celibacy may not be the same as those in marriage, but it would be hard to prove that they are any greater. The Rule of Taizé calls each brother to 'open himself to all that is human', and speaks of celibacy only as a road to greater openness and love, for the sake of Christ:

'Celibacy brings greater freedom to attend to the things of

God, but it can only be accepted with the aim of giving ourselves more completely to our neighbour with the love of Christ himself.

'Our celibacy means neither indifference nor a break with human affections; it calls for their transfiguration. Christ alone can convert our passions into total love of our neighbour. When selfishness is not transcended by growing generosity, when you no longer resort to confession to overcome the need for self-assertion contained in every passion, when the heart is not constantly brimming over with great love, you can no longer let Christ love in you, and your celibacy becomes a burden.

'Purity of heart can only be lived in spontaneous, joyful self-forgetting, as we give our lives for those we love. Giving ourselves in this way means accepting that our susceptibilities will often be wounded.

'There is no friendship without purifying suffering.

'There is no love for our neighbour without the Cross. Only by the Cross can we know the unfathomable depths of love.'

N.B. Quotations from the Rule of Taizé in this chapter are taken from the 1984 edition entitled *Parable of Community: Basic Texts of Taizé*. In 1990, to mark the fiftieth anniversay of his arrival in Taizé, Brother Roger undertook a major updating of 'les sources de Taizé', published under the title *No Greater Love: Sources of Taizé*.

The Challenge

CAN YOU tell me of any other place in the world today that continually attracts so many young adults, from so many different countries, with such a variety of backgrounds and occupations, for such a serious purpose, offering such rudimentary conditions? Why Taizé? Of course the landscape is beautiful, with the red roofs of the stone houses snuggling below the slender tower of the old church. Across the valley on every side rise hills clothed with fields, forests and vineyards. Often the only sound to be heard is the shrilling of countless grasshoppers. Yet Assisi or Montserrat are more dramatically beautiful and no less silent. But it happens to be Taizé. People arrive in this out-of-the-way place by hundreds and thousands, throughout the year.

There are people for whom every country outside their own is 'abroad' – implying holidays and escapism. But Taizé is no holiday-camp, and you are strongly discouraged from treating it as one. This does not exclude the atmosphere of real joy and celebration that usually reigns. The singing of the common prayer tells you that: *Jubilate Deo . . . Surrexit Christus alleluia*! But the joy of the meetings rarely evaporates into superficial euphoria: if the festival proposed is so real, it is because it does not urge people to be other than they really are or to forget the pain of the world. It is not a mask of pretence, but encounters in truth. The first encounter is that 'inner pilgrimage' within ourselves; from that flows the pilgrimage outward, the encounter with others. Even if you only know three words of the other person's language.

The celebration of life offered in Taizé involves sharing

one another's burdens and hopes in the awareness of our common struggles. The differences may be enormous: Spaniards do not think like English people, Italians and Swedes do not sing the same songs, Poles and Latin Americans may not have the same expectations of the Church. Yet the festive encounter lies beyond these factors; it is a common search for the living presence of Christ who is love and who gives meaning to all our struggles. When masks can be set aside because trust is born, when our human poverty ceases to be something to conceal, then we can advance towards true communion. Then, perhaps, we discover something of what the Church is called to be: a place of communion for all, a leaven of trust and peace at the heart of the human family.

Why Taizé? Perhaps, though it is hardly a sufficient answer for any sociologist, because here a group of men living together without any reserves, rooted in contemplation, constantly strives to draw nearer to God and nearer to their brothers and sisters in one and the same movement.

There, at least, lies one fundamental aspect of the challenge Taizé offers. Here are people who pray, and who are alert to news arriving from every continent, be it a drought in Africa, or a coup d'état elsewhere, a riot in India, troubles in Bangladesh, or a guerilla leader sentenced to death without trial in Latin America. Good news too, of new possibilities, of dictatorships toppling, of hope reborn. . . . In the common prayer morning and evening you hear people and situations being brought before God, and suddenly you realise that this is communion; it is an expression of concern and at the same time 'a sharing in the suffering of Christ for his Body'. The whole celebration of God in prayer here is full of this challenge to 'live the communion Christ offers and so become people of communion for others'. Silence and beauty, a space of contemplation, the Church of Reconciliation welcomes you, with the sunlight streaming in golden patterns down the walls, or in the silent darkness of evening. Small lights draw your gaze towards the altar, to the icon of Mary, to the tabernacle. The bells peal, songs fill the silence, then release it again – a long pause holding us all together in the heart of God. On Sunday morning the Eucharist, culmination of the week, a sharing in Christ's Body and Blood. Late at night you will still find people in church, in prayer, prostrate and simply waiting.

Why Taizé? The young people here seem to know that nobody is playing tricks on them. If people pray in Taizé, they know that it is not in order to run away from today's world. If questions of peace and justice are given a place in the discussion-groups that more inward-oriented Christians find disconcerting, still the celebration of Christ remains the central pivot around which all else turns. Not 'either the world or Christ' but 'the whole of humanity because of Christ'.

'But define your terms.' 'Be more precise.' 'What do you really mean when you say that?' – We are all the time trying to tie people down and fit them into our own snug, static framework of ideas. But meanwhile, in the world around us, life goes on; people are divided from one another; there are urgent challenges addressed to us. To reconcile, to bring communion into situations where there is distrust and to heal the divisions so that life can evolve: none of that is easy. It is far easier to divide by opposing and comparing things and people: 'right or wrong', 'good or bad', 'clever or stupid', 'success or failure'. What of the other way, that of welcoming, trying to keep opposites together? Ambiguous? Often to the point of anguish. It is only possible when we are clear that we want that and nothing else. Necessarily ambiguous and unsure, the way of reconciliation is a narrow path leading forwards. Tensions lie to either side, but along that way lies communion – with Christ and with others, with all. The movement of people along that path is the true

116

'story of Taizé', its secret history. But who could ever write it?

So life, and Taizé, continue. The challenge is there. Only this book has to end. . . .

TO LEARN MORE ABOUT TAIZÉ

1. Books by Brother Roger

His Love Is A Fire
Central writings with extracts from journals
Australia & New Zealand: St Paul Publications, 60 Broughton Road, Homebush, NSW 2140. Philippines: Claretian Publications, Quezon City. UK: Geoffrey Chapman Mowbray, Stanley House, Fleets Lane, Poole BH15 3A5. USA & Canada: The Liturgical Press, St John's Abbey, Collegeville, MN 56321.

Life From Within
Prayers by Brother Roger and icons from the Church of Reconciliation
UK: Geoffrey Chapman Mowbray. USA: Westminster Press.

And Your Deserts Shall Flower (Journal 1977–79)
UK: Mowbray
A Heart That Trusts (Journal 1979–81)
UK: Mowbray

2. By Mother Teresa and Brother Roger

Meditations On The Way Of The Cross
India: Asian Trading Corporation, Bangalore. UK: Mowbray. USA: The Pilgrim Press.

Mary, Mother Of Reconciliations
Australia & New Zealand: St Paul. India: Daughters of St Paul, Bombay. Philippines: Claretian. UK: Mowbray. USA: Paulist Press, Mahwah, NJ.

3. About Taizé

The Taizé Experience
A book of photographs by Vladimir Sichov with texts by
Brother Roger
UK: Mowbray. USA & Canada: Liturgical Press.

Taizé – Trust Is At Hand
28 minute VHS PAL video-cassette.
The community and the intercontinental meetings, both in
Taizé and elsewhere – in European capitals, Madras,
Brother Roger at UNESCO, etc.
Australia & New Zealand: Rainbow Book Agencies, 134
Emmaline Street, PO Box 58, Northcote, Vic 3070. UK:
Mowbray.

A Pilgrimage Of Trust On Earth
Colour booklet with photographs and texts about the com-
munity and the meetings in Taizé.
UK: Mowbray.

4. Preparing Prayers in Parishes and Groups

Praying Together In Word And Song
Booklet with suggestions for prayer together and a selection
of Brother Roger's prayers.
UK: Mowbray. USA: GIA, 7407 S. Mason Avenue,
Chicago, Ill 60638.

Music From Taizé
Two volumes. Vocal & instrumental editions.
Australia: Dove Communications, PO Box 316, Blackburn,
Vic 3130. UK: Collins Liturgical. USA: GIA.

5. Music Cassettes

Canons Et Litanies – Cantate – Alleluia (also on CD) – *Resurrexit* (also on CD)
Australia: Rainbow Book Agencies, Northcote, Vic. UK: All main stores; distribution: Auvidis, 39, av Paul Vaillant Couturier, F–94250 Gentilly. USA: GIA.

6. The Letter From Taizé
Published every two months in fifteen languages, news from across the world, themes for group reflection, texts for meditation, prayers and daily Bible readings – Subscriptions: write to Taizé.

* * *

* Geoffrey Chapman Mowbray books are distributed in Australia by Canterbury Press Ltd, Unit 2, 7 Rusdale Street, Scoresby, Vic 3179; in Canada by Meakin Associates, Unit 17, 81 Auriga Drive, Nepean, Ontario K2E 7Y5; in New Zealand: Hodder & Stoughton, PO 3858, Auckland; in South Africa by Century Hutchinson, PO 337 Bergvlei, 20125.

To Reach Taizé

By road: Coming from the North on the Autoroute A6, turn off at Chalon-Sud or Tournus. Coming from the South, turn off at Mâcon-Sud.

By rail: Either train to Chalon-sur-Saône or Mâcon-Ville; or high speed train (TGV) to Mâcon-Loché. The connecting but service on the Chalon-Taizé-Cluny-Mâcon line is part of the rail network (SNCF timetable no.576). Taizé is a station on this line, so tickets direct to Taizé are obtainable, covering both train and bus parts of the journey.

Coach service from London: At half-term, Easter, and June to September, overnight coaches to Taizé run weekly from London. Write to Taizé for details.

The meetings in Taizé are intended mainly for young adults between 17 and 30. Living conditions are very simple.

Adults over 30 are welcome for one week in the quieter months of April, May, June, September or October.

Parents with children at Easter, Pentecost and from late June to early September. Families form a group in a house specially reserved for them.

* * *

For more information, contact:
The Taizé Community,
71250 Cluny, France.

* For the Community:
  Telephone: (France = 33) 85.50.30.30

* For the Meetings:
Direct line for information and registration for the meetings in English. From Monday to Friday and Saturday mornings:

> From 10am to 12 noon (French time)
> From 4.30 to 6.30pm (French time)

Telephone: (33) 85.50.30.02

* Telex: 800753F COTAIZE
* Fax: (33) 85.50.30.15

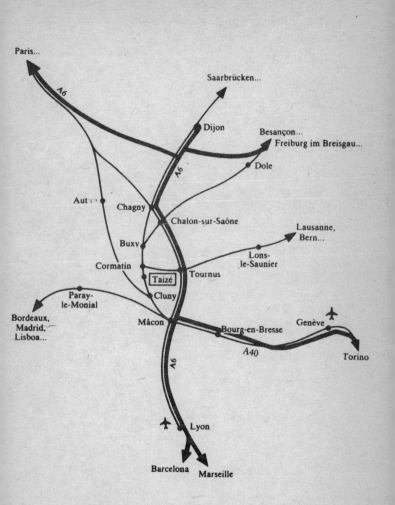

Paris...

Saarbrücken...

A6

Dijon

Besançon...
Freiburg im Breisgau...

A6

Dole

Autun

Chagny

Chalon-sur-Saône

Lausanne,
Bern...

Buxy

Cormatin

Lons-
le-Saunier

Taizé

Tournus

Paray-
le-Monial

Cluny

Bordeaux,
Madrid,
Lisboa...

Mâcon

Bourg-en-Bresse

Genève

A6

A40

Torino

Lyon

Barcelona   Marseille

123